Praise for BELONGING

"An interesting mix of memoir, short story and travelogue . . .
A book about the yearning to belong, family ties, unexpected
friendships and how life usually turns out to be quite different from our plans, it's a pleasure to read and provides an
intimate look at a fascinating and open-minded woman."
—*The Toronto Sun*

"The book is part engaging memoir and part intriguing explo-
ration of how the creative mind works."
—*Winnipeg Free Press*

"Summer reading, I believe, should either draw you forcefully
out of your world, or draw you irresistibly further into it.
Belonging may do both. . . . This is not so much a book to read,
as to re-read. Huggan's stories [are] graced with turns of
phrase and pockets of language that, well, make you turn
down the page to go back." —*The Observer*

"The best part of this book is her candid and engaging voice.
By the time you turn the page on the last memoir in the collection, you feel welcomed as a friend, made privy to confi-
dences, epiphanic insights and intimate memories."
—*Ottawa Citizen*

"*Belonging* is an elegant, gracefully written reminiscence of
what it means to leave your home and native land. . . . It's an
entrancing journey." —*The Sun Times*

Home Away from Home

Belonging

Isabel Huggan

VINTAGE CANADA

VINTAGE CANADA EDITION, 2004

Copyright © 2003 Isabel Huggan

Published in Canada by Vintage Canada, a division of Random House of Canada
Limited, Toronto. Originally published in hardcover in Canada by Alfred A. Knopf
Canada, a division of Random House of Canada Limited, Toronto, in 2003.
Distributed by Random House of Canada Limited, Toronto.

Vintage Canada and colophon are registered trademarks of
Random House of Canada Limited.

In the nonfiction section of this book, several names have been changed to maintain
the privacy of individuals; in the fiction, however, all characters bear their own names.

Some of these essays and stories have appeared in earlier and different versions.
See page 333, which constitutes a continuation of the copyright page,
for publishing history.

NATIONAL LIBRARY OF CANADA CATALOGUING IN PUBLICATION

Huggan, Isabel, 1943–
Belonging : home away from home / Isabel Huggan.

ISBN 0-676-97538-0

I. Title.

PS8565.U33B34 2004   c813'.54   C2003-905681-3

www.randomhouse.ca

Printed and bound in Canada

2 4 6 8 9 7 5 3

For Ann,
who sees me through

ACKNOWLEDGMENTS

My primary and most heartfelt thanks go to my family —my sister Ruth, my daughter Abbey, and above all, my husband Bob whose love and support is so crucial to my life and work.

I am deeply grateful to Louise Dennys, Bella Pomer and Susan Roxborough for their affectionate loyalty over the years and for their steadfast conviction that this book would be written. Working with Louise to shape *Belonging* has been wonderful.

I owe a great deal to Joe Kertes and the Humber School for Writers for providing me with an ongoing connection and commitment to Canada. Sincere appreciation goes also to the Tasmanian Writers' Centre and the Hobart City

Council for my residency in 2001. Without the financial assistance of the Canadian Government when I was first invited to Australia, I would not have discovered Tasmania, where I have enjoyed such warm hospitality. There are too many kind people to thank individually, but an exception must be made for Gillian Johnson and Nicholas Shakespeare who let me use their beach house.

Ever since I left Canada in 1987, Robert and Carol Lovejoy have given me a home in Ottawa each summer, helping to maintain the happy illusion that I've never really gone away. My love and gratitude for their generous friendship grows with every passing year.

I am indebted to several friends for their thoughtful criticism and sustaining companionship through email. These include Robert Dessaix, the remaining Audreys (Sheila McCook and Elizabeth Hay) and Jon Miller. Special thanks are due Danielle Breton and Sandy Forbes, who supplied this book with its title.

For many years, Carol Shields has encouraged and inspired me: *Belonging* is my way of saying thank you.

Do you understand the sadness of geography?
MICHAEL ONDAATJE, The English Patient

So we are caught stumbling
in between, longing for home.
....
Only in fairy tales,
or given freakish luck, does the wind
rise suddenly and set you down where everything
is safe and loved and in its place. The mind
does not expect it. But the heart,

the heart—
the heart keeps looking for itself.
It knows and does not know
where it belongs.

JAN ZWICKY, "Transparence,"
Songs for Relinquishing the Earth

Home makes possible the possession of the world.
DON MCKAY, "Baler Twine," Vis à Vis

CONTENTS

There Is No Word for Home   1

Saving Stones   23

Graceland   34

Going to Banaue   66

Someday You'll Be Sorry   83

Hard of Happiness   115

Fire   134

Snow   156

Learning to Wait   161

Rain   176

Learning to Talk   191

Homage to Kenko   209

Making Up Mother   226

Fast Water, Slow Love   245

S.E.M.A.P.H.O.R.E.   270

The Window   281

Arnica   295

Starting with the Chair   314

THERE IS NO WORD FOR HOME

IN THE COUNTRY WHERE I now live, there is no word for home. You can express the idea at a slant, but you cannot say *home*. For a long time this disconcerted me, and I kept running up against the lack as if it were a rock in my path, worse than a pothole, worse than nothing. But at last I have habituated myself and can step around it, using variants such as *notre foyer* (our hearth) or *notre maison* (our house) when I mean to say home. More often, I use the concept *chez* to indicate physical location and the place where family resides, or the notion of a comfortable domestic space. However, if I wish to speak of "going home to Canada," I can use *mon pays* (my country) but I can't say I am going *chez moi* when I am not: for as long as I reside in France—the rest of my life—this is where I will be *chez moi*, making a home in a country and a language not my own. I am both home and not-home, one of those trick syllogisms I must solve by homemaking, at an age when I should have finished with all that bother.

In the foothills of the Cévennes I live in a stone house that was, until only a few decades ago, home to silkworms, hundreds upon hundreds of them, squirming in flat reed baskets laid on layered frames along the walls in what was then the *magnanerie,* a place for feeding silkworms, and is now a bedroom. For the duration of their brief lives, these slippery dun-coloured creatures munched mulberry leaves, fattening themselves sufficiently to shed their skins four times before they'd stop eating and attach themselves to twigs or sprigs of heather on racks above the baskets. With a sense of purpose sprung from genetic necessity, they'd then spin themselves cocoons in which they'd sleep until they were plucked from their branches and dunked in huge kettles of hot water. Perhaps some luckier ones were allowed to waken and complete the magic of metamorphosis—there must be moths, after all, to furnish next season's eggs—but silk manufacturers preferred the longer filament, which comes from whole cocoons. There are sacrifices to be made for beauty, and if the life of a lowly and not very attractive segmented grub has to be that sacrifice, perhaps that is the Lord's will.

The Lord's will rests heavy on the high blue hills of the Cévennes, for here God has been imagined in

Calvinist clothes, a moral master whose plans for man and beast alike are stern. This little-inhabited part of southern France (the mountainous northern corner of Languedoc, much of it now a national park) has long been the heart of Protestant opposition to Roman Catholicism. From the mid-1500s, revolt against Paris and the Church continued with appropriate bloodshed on all sides until the *Édit de Tolérance* in 1787 finally allowed those few Huguenots who remained the right to practise their religion.

The rugged terrain, hidden valleys and craggy cliffs are geologically congenial to the Protestant mind—in the back reaches of the Cévennes there have always existed stubborn pockets of religious and political resistance. This is an austere landscape where, even now, life is not taken lightly and where pleasure and ease are distrusted. The puritanical harshness of Reform doctrine seems also to show itself in the fortress-like architecture of Huguenot houses such as mine: angular, stiff-necked buildings, tall and narrow with small windows shuttered against the blasts of winter or the blaze of summer. Nevertheless, graceless and severe though it may appear from outside, the cool, dark interior of the house is a blessing when you step in from the painful dazzle of an August day. It is not for nothing that the stone walls are well over half a metre thick, or that the floors are laid with glazed clay tiles.

Sometimes I wake in the early morning before it is light, the still, dark hours of silent contemplation: how have I come to be here? But there is nothing mysterious, the reason is mundane—it is not the will of God, but the wish of the Scottish-born man to whom I have been married since 1970. The first time we came hiking in these mountains—more than a decade ago, while we were living in Montpellier—he said, immediately, that he knew he was *chez lui dans les Cévennes*. His experience was profound, affecting him in some deeply atavistic way I did not understand until later, when I felt the same inexpressible, magnetic, and nearly hormonal pull the moment I first set foot in Tasmania and knew myself to be home.

When it happens, this carnal knowledge of landscape, it is very like falling in love without knowing why, the plunge into desire and longing made all the more intense by being so utterly irrational, inexplicable. The feel of the air, the lay of the land, the colour and shape of the horizon, who knows? There are places on the planet we belong and they are not necessarily where we are born. If we are lucky—if the gods are in a good mood—we find them, for whatever length of time is necessary for us to know that, yes, we belong to the earth and it to us. Even if we cannot articulate this intense physical sensation, even if language fails us, we know what home is then, in our very bones.

I sometimes say jokingly that I have become a WTGW—a whither-thou-goest-wife, an almost extinct species, but one with which I have become intimately familiar in the years we have lived abroad because of Bob's work in development. I have met many other spouses—men, as well as women—who have done the same as I: we have weighed the choices, and we have followed our partners. Our reasons for doing so are as diverse as our marriages and our aspirations and the work that we do. In my case, writing is a portable occupation: I can do what I do anywhere.

And so it follows that I shall learn, as I have learned in other places, to make this house home. Over time, I shall find out how to grow in and be nourished by this rocky foreign soil. I early learn the phrase *je m'enracine ici,* which means "I am putting down roots here," in order to convince myself—for this time, we are not moving on. We are here to stay, *définitivement.*

The house, Mas Blanc, is one of ninety other scattered farms and hamlets that constitute the commune of Latourne. The property we bought includes a stone barn and a hectare of land beside the little river Ourne—a few old olive trees, a field we're making into an orchard, and part of the bush-covered hillside along our lane, where we gather deadwood for kindling. Mas means "farmhouse" and can designate either a single dwelling or a collection of buildings grouped together: over a couple of centuries, the central house, which is ours, extended itself in a manner not unlike the Mennonite farmhouses in Waterloo county where I grew up, with various stone outbuildings attaching themselves as part of the whole. Possession of this property has changed hands many times, until today the house and its various parcels of land are divided among three owners. We know, from a document dated 1646, that this was one of nine farms belonging to the Duchy of Latourne for which the family seat was a hilltop castle, now in ruins, about two kilometres away. Along with the others, Mas Blanc still bears the name it was given then, and we could never change it, even if we were so inclined. By chance, the stones from which the house is built are a light creamy colour, but we believe that the place was named for a family called Blanc, and not because it is white.

Within Latourne, various sections of the commune have specific names, some of them springing from location and others from historical connection. Our portion is known as La Grenouille, probably because the nearby Ourne and its two millponds are a perfect breeding ground for frogs. Big, plump, noisy frogs. Beginning in April and continuing through the summer, the nightly racket they make is less than charming if you are trying to sleep, but as the presence of frogs indicates an absence of pollution, we philosophically bear their creaking and honking. When we first bought the house, we were so amused to have something froggy as

part of our address that we included it on everything—only to discover that the word *grenouille* is
hellishly difficult to pronounce correctly. We've given
it up, although the phone book continues to list it
properly after our name.

The Ourne separates us from vineyards that once
belonged to the nearby monastery, an assemblage of
tall stone buildings divided long ago among four
families who have left part in ruins and renovated the
rest for their own use. Church records in Nîmes at the
end of the eighth century mention the Monastère de
St-Étienne and in 808 A.D., when Charlemagne was
passing through this region, he is said to have stopped
by and taken mass. No doubt one of those "X slept
here" tales, nevertheless the fact that it could possibly
be true is enough to cloak the entire area in the rich
sauce of history. Why should this make living here
more palatable? But it does.

One winter's day last year I noticed a man with a
metal detector in the vineyard along the road and,
when I asked what he was looking for, was told,
"Roman coins." Although he appeared to be a rough
type—shaggy hair, ruddy face, ill-fitting old clothes,
the sort of fellow you see selling junk at flea markets—
he was kindness itself and took time to give me a pocket version of local history, the ebb and flow of Celts,
Greeks, Romans, Goths, Saracens—you name them,
they were here, and they left their mark everywhere.

He lifted a chunk of rose-brown brick from the soil and gave it to me: "Roman," he said. No more Roman than I am, I thought, but I took it graciously and carried it home, a reminder that everywhere around me there are bits and pieces of the past, visible and invisible. In *Lives of a Cell*, Lewis Thomas said, "We leave traces of ourselves wherever we go, on whatever we touch." Perfume lingering in the air, letters in the attic, the pressure of your hand on the small of my back as we danced, tears on the pillow, a shard of pottery, a piece of brick.

There's an apricot-coloured brick above the doorway of our barn, on which is carved 1853, the same year a boatload of my poor Scottish ancestors began settling themselves down on the shores of Lake Huron, thrown off their heathery land in the Hebrides for the sake of sheep. Seemed a long time ago, 1853, when I was growing up in Canada: seems yesterday, here. The barn is considered relatively new, and even our house, built well over a century before that, is not considered *old:* old is reserved for the Château de Latourne, built over the remains of a Roman tower and in ruins since being burned at the beginning of the Revolution. Old is St-Baudile, a stone church built for the parish of Latourne by the monks of St-Étienne in the twelfth century: I can see it from my window, plain and chaste in the middle of vineyards, a perfect little *église romane* guarded by a stand of cypress.

Time passes unevenly from place to place, has different weight and value. Here, it seems to have collapsed, folding in and compressing itself into something deep and dense, a richer, thicker brew than I, a child of the New World, have been accustomed to. The air I breathe as I walk by the Ourne is full of old souls, the noise of the water falling over the dam is like the sound of distant voices. Layer upon layer of lives come and gone.

In Canada, it is easy to keep one's childish illusions of primordial nature intact when out in the woods, whether canoeing through the bush in Algonquin Park or taking a Sunday stroll through autumn-stained maples in the Gatineau hills. In our heads, even as adults, we can continue to play "explorer" and deceive ourselves that we are surrounded by untouched wilderness. Hiking in the Cévennes, one finds different games to play, games of retrieval, understanding one's place in the context of others. Just a few metres from the path, a ruined stone wall will emerge, moss covered and beautiful, in the midst of forest that, until this moment, has seemed pristine. There have been so many other people here before me, and the tangible evidence of that raises questions, gives me pause, thrills me to my boots.

Why should bits of brick and stone be so seductive? The people who passed through this land have nothing to do with me: this is not my story. Nevertheless, I am touched by the past and stand with tears in my eyes reading a plaque at a mountain pass commemorating the deaths of seven local partisans in the Resistance: the heroes in the Cévennes have been *camisard* and *maquis,* resistance fighters in every century. Near Anduze, the village where we go to market, there stands a memorial to the destruction of a German Army brigade in 1944 by local *maquis:* courage, death, victory, freedom. All the big notions, over and over again, on the same ground.

In much the same way as I read Susanna Moodie's 1853 memoir *Life in the Clearings* when we moved from Toronto to Belleville, because I passed her old stone cottage every day on my way to work and felt I should pay literary homage, I spend much time reading books about this region to learn who was here when, and why, slowly getting a sense of how things fit together. And just as the Victorian sensibilities of Moodie's prose had little to do with my life in 1972, nothing I read now seems directly relevant to my immediate task. Nothing I read will ever make me fit here. I will always be an outsider, no matter how much history I swallow. Nevertheless, I persist, imbued as I am with the belief that reading is the way to salvation.

Throughout this region, emptied of people for reasons as various as war, famine and financial failure, there are terraced hillsides on which mulberry trees once flourished. Although some terraces are used today for growing olive trees or onions, most of them are abandoned and overgrown, melancholy testimony to change and loss. In the rafters of our barn we found bunches of old mulberry branches, the leaves dry and brown, left behind after the raising of silkworms was no longer profitable even as a cottage industry. Most of the silk factories in the Cévennes had already closed by the end of the nineteenth century but some farmers continued to use the upper part of their houses as *magnaneries* until the 1940s, when silk was still used for parachutes.

Measuring time by the remembrance of Fanette, one of five elderly local women who once came for tea, it seems that was true in my house. Fanette, well over seventy, recalls being in this house as a child—she was born round the corner in the monastery—and when I took her and the others on a tour of the house to see our renovations, she threw up her hands in astonishment as we entered the bedroom, recalling how it had looked when the *vieille dame Augustine* had lived here and kept her *vers à soie* upstairs. "*Alors, quelle différence,*" she said, shaking her head in disbelief.

The ladies came to tea with my friend the widow Germaine, as I'd suggested she bring the companions with whom she walks for exercise on Tuesdays. When they arrived at the door they were buzzing with curiosity, as if an electric current were lighting up their lovely old faces: unheard of in this rural community to be invited in and allowed to look through someone's house. What a grand opportunity! How amazing is this Canadian! In the village the week after, I heard it was said, in tones not of censure but delight, *Elle est très ouverte!*

Germaine is very fond of me, she says. Two years earlier when I arrived in June for the summer, she met me on the road and told me that over the winter her husband, Armand, had died. Surprised by the news, I burst into tears and we wept together, arms round each other, both of us moved by the other's sadness. At that moment, she says, we became friends. He was a lovely man, Armand, with bright blue eyes, a big white moustache and wine-red cheeks, and he kept the little mill, just the other side of the stone bridge that leads to our long lane. He, and his father and grandfather before him, had turned out whole-grain flour for well over a century until the mill was ruined in the flood of October 1995, when the Ourne, normally a shallow stream, overnight roared swollen and crazy and turned into a torrent carrying trees and horses and cars in its rushing course. The horses are dead and gone, but uprooted trunks and rusting fenders lodged for years along its banks, like mournful memories, reminders that flood and drought are a double scourge in this countryside.

I met Germaine and Armand the first summer we arrived to work on the old house—we were living in the Philippines then. Although we didn't bother getting a telephone for that short time, it was no hardship as there's a public booth at the *mairie,* only a ten-minute walk away. One evening, on my way to make a call, I came upon Germaine with her old bicycle on the road by the monastery. After my polite *"Bonsoir, madame,"* she struck up a conversation, evidently curious about who I was and what we were doing at Mas Blanc. Once her questions were answered, she offered the use of the telephone in her small apartment in the monastery.

Somewhere in her sixties, with short hair hennaed that deep purple shade favoured by Frenchwomen, Germaine has a sharpness to her features I now recognize as typically Cévenole but at the time found slightly forbidding. She insisted I meet Armand, who was in the monastery gardens, planting beans. We shook hands and then I offered to help and he accepted, after being assured that I knew the right way to plant: three beans to a hill. As darkness fell upon us and the stars came out and bats joined the swooping martins overhead, we worked up and down the rows, me chatting away in cheerful high-school French, sticking beans in the soil, patting them down, planting them and myself in this place. And now Armand is dead and the mill stays ruined and empty, for his son never learned the trade, and Germaine has given up their section of the monastery and lives alone in a nearby hamlet.

Everything, for me, dates from that hour of planting beans. The familiar rhythm, the smell of damp earth, somehow knowing where I was because I was in a garden. Lines from a poem by Margaret Avison, memorized more than thirty years ago, resonate with new meaning now: "When day and life draw the horizons, / Part of the strangeness is / Knowing the landscape." There are moments I startle myself nearly witless because I sense so acutely where I am, know exactly the curve of the road and where to slow down, or when to expect the sunlight to catch itself in the crystal prism hanging in the window, or which way to turn to find Orion's Belt in the clear night sky. Emotional geometry, physical knowledge of the deepest sort, the kind that resides under the skin beneath history, beyond words.

During these years spent outside Canada, I've lived by something I read in an interview with surgeon Chris Giannou: "Home is not a physical, geographic entity. Home is a moral state. The real home is one's friends. I like to think of that as a higher form of social organization than the nation state." With my parents dead and no home to return to in Canada, I found this gave me great comfort in our expatriate years abroad, for I kept in mind the idea that we were "only renting temporarily" because of Bob's work, and my real home was somewhere else, invisible but enduring—and permanent.

But something in me is changing. I am burrowing down into an actual place now, my hands in the dirt, planting tulip and narcissus bulbs under the spreading branches of the old *micocoulier*, the wild nettle tree that stands by the house. It is the feel of the earth I desire, this most primitive need finding expression in an act as simple as digging holes and plunking in bulbs. Has this to do with growing older, approaching the earth itself on new terms? Perhaps. Bent on one knee, I let the leafy humus run through my fingers, wondering if I might be buried here someday, whether I want to be, or not. We are told there are already three dead Protestants under the barn, interred two hundred years ago according to a local ordinance that allowed home burial for non-Catholics. If I still lived in Canada, would I occupy myself with questions about where my bones or ashes will go? This is a sign, no doubt, that my heart feels in exile, no matter how I try to force these bulbs into the ground. But I do not dwell on such foolish thoughts for long—it is autumn and I am busy preparing for spring. What better indication of an optimistic spirit could there be?

Much of my effort here so far has gone toward supervising interior renovations, such as the installation of a bathroom and a kitchen, making the place habitable and, more than that, homey. Good plumbing and carpentry are required, but small things matter too, like bouquets of wildflowers on the table. And in the first months, it is less the house than the surrounding hills to which I attach myself, walking daily and learning to name those wildflowers. I am discovering this small truth: to feel *chez vous*, you need to know the proper names for things. Thus I must rename daisies *marguerites*, call the swallows *hirondelles* and the chestnut tree *châtaignier*. It is work, pure and simple. And it is daunting. My mouth cannot produce the liquid sounds required by the French language, my throat cannot give up a rounded *r*, my tongue cannot do arabesques around the word *heureuse*, my lips purse up to no avail.

And my ears! I live in a muddled state of mild incomprehension, often uncertain if I have properly grasped what has been said: my public stance is one of brave bewilderment, my tone of voice inquiring, apologetic. In some ways I exist at a level beneath language, where words do not touch me, but at the same time I am forever trying to "catch on," to know and be known. I am not myself, at the same time as I am more myself than ever, for there is also constant clear definition. I am visibly not French. I am sometimes taken for Dutch or American, and then I explain that *je suis Canadienne anglophone*. I will always be foreign, alien, *toujours une étrangère*.

When I am in Toronto on my annual teaching visit, sitting in a subway car amused and amazed at the wonderful way the faces of the city have changed since I lived in a boarding house on St. George Street in 1965, I think how hard it is to learn another language, to get it right, to make yourself fit to the shape of different sounds in your mouth. I want to tell the woman beside me—Cambodian, Peruvian, Ethiopian, Croatian—*I know how you feel. It's not easy. It's lonely and tough. But trust me, start with little things: flowers, trees, birds. Make a little garden, if only in your head. Get to know your neighbours. Dream of home and it will come to you.*

But then I think how incredibly presumptuous it would be to offer such platitudes, and I do not reach out, I stay silent. What can I possibly know of her plight? Why should she care that I, who appear to belong in this city, also know what it's like to be an outsider? What earthly good might it do? What works for me may work for no one else.

Get to know your neighbours. For me, that's made easy because Mas Blanc is divided in three and we all exist within its walls. My house is the central one and, jutting off to one side, rather like the half stroke of a nearly crossed *t,* is the section belonging to Bruno, a professional comedian. In the summer he and the other two members of his troupe practise their act on a small stage in his yard, and I sit on my front steps to watch, not getting the jokes, which rely on wordplay or political satire, but applauding their hilarious slapstick routines. Bruno is a small, trim man whose mobile facial features can seem comic even in repose: just now, watching him walk to the mailbox, I find myself smiling, for he has the flat-footed gait of a clown.

More important, he has something to teach me about appearance and reality. At first, I found myself appalled by his disregard for what he terms middle-class values: the old cement-block outhouse in his unkempt front yard seemed so ugly, I kept waiting for him to "fix things up" and get rid of it, but it is apparent the outhouse is here to stay. If it's good enough weather for outdoor chores, he's off on his *vélo*, cycling for the entire day, coming back at nightfall exhausted and joyous. To Bruno, what matters is not how things look, but whether life is good.

The outhouse remains an eyesore but, as time passes, I am seeing the wisdom of his point of view. Bruno is not only a content man but a generous and kindly neighbour without whom life would be dull. He fires the ancient wood-burning oven attached to our barn, and we bake bread and pizza. He fixes my bicycle tires, offers advice when I am stymied by the linguistic convolutions of French bureaucracy, and he'll feed our cat, Ballou, if we're away. Last week he brought us a bag of *girolles*, wild yellow mushrooms that taste like the very first time you heard Chopin.

At the rear, there is an addition that would form the top of the *t*, home to a family whose big, rambling garden runs along the entire Mas on the side nearest the stream. Haddou is a friendly man in his late forties, but conversation with him is difficult because he is missing some teeth and, perhaps out of embarrassment, he bends his head and speaks rapidly. Malika, his plump, pretty wife, embraces me each time we meet, but is shy about speaking French, so we are limited mainly to smiles and gestures. They have five children—the younger ones, Leila and Hakim, still in grade school and the elder three trying to find work. Haddou and Malika are Moroccan, and they know even better than I what it is to live in a land where you are never completely accepted, although they've been here more than half their lives.

We do not talk of this so much as acknowledge it in sideways fashion, discussing the problems of getting jobs as I sit at their round table drinking sweet mint tea or strong black coffee, listening to the frustrations faced by the teenage girls, Sonya and Saphira, and their older brother, Hassan. I do what I can to help, driving them to interviews and typing their brief résumés, but in a region where unemployment is endemic and where there is underlying support and sympathy for Le Pen and his xenophobic National Front party, what colour your skin is and where your parents come from matter more than what your curriculum vitae looks like.

Haddou has worked twenty years in the vineyards of Béatrice, a middle-aged single woman with a boyish, bashful manner, who always wears a delicate gold chain and Huguenot cross even with her farm clothes. It is she who owns that section of Mas Blanc, and she allows Haddou to live there as part of his salary. On her farm, over the hill, Béatrice keeps goats and in good weather, if she is not occupied tending her vines, can be found striding out with her small herd and her dogs. Aided by her frail old father—in his nineties now, his help more token than real—she makes goats' cheese (called *pelardon*), which she sells from her home.

There, in the first room of the little cheese shed, sit snowy-white rounds of *pelardon,* so creamy and delicate that they are delicious eaten with fresh strawberries or figs. At the back of the shed are cheeses in various stages of maturity, becoming more dense and yellow with each week they spend on the airing rack. Béatrice's specialty is a very old cheese dried to half its original size, dark blue with mold and hard as rock, aged with herbs in a stoneware jar. For this, she gives me the following traditional Cévenol recipe: grate the cheese into a bowl and add the same amount of fresh butter and finely chopped walnuts. Mix well and serve on slices of warm baguette. Washed down with ice-cold rosé wine from the *Cave Coopérative*—the winery where, every September, she and Haddou take the grapes they've picked in the vineyard behind our house—this is sustenance of an elemental sort, tasting of this earth, this rain and sun, this air. This place where I live.

As I write this, intending to describe a middle-aged Canadian settling into the rhythms of rural France, it is obvious that I am seeking to convince myself, choosing words that will chase ambivalence into the shadows. A line floats into my head, so perfectly appropriate that it makes me laugh aloud: "If you can't be with the one you love, then love the one you're with." Easier said than done, of course. I know all about homesickness—sipping maple syrup from a spoon while listening to a tape cassette of loon calls, endlessly writing letters to friends asking for news, sifting through old photographs, weeping on the telephone. I've been there, that strange and dangerous place where longing can blind you to everything else. And so you learn to live with *mal de pays* as with a chronic illness or disability, you salt your days with *nostalgie*. Then finally you wake up and compare yourself to the millions of displaced people in the world who will never see their homes again, and you feel ashamed, and you stop.

You go for a walk in the hills and watch a hawk unwinding on an updraft. You know this hawk, he has a certain territory and he is part of the landscape you now know like the back of your hand. Or you put on gardening gloves and take your trowel and another bag of tulip bulbs and work at making a garden, while the falling leaves of the *micocoulier* land on your shoulders like rain. At night you fall into bed content that you are creating whatever it is that is *chez vous*.

The ghosts of the silkworms are as silent as they were in life, and you sleep without interruption, except for the hourly tolling of the bell at the *mairie* coming clear and sweet across the fields. It always rings the hour twice, as if to ensure that its message is heard: Listen, it says. Pay attention. This is where you are.

SAVING STONES

THE FIRST STONES seemed big to my seven-year-old hands, shining black with the cold water of Lake Huron still dripping through my fingers as I held them up to the sun. We walked along the beach, my father and I, keeping our eyes on the stones and pebbles and shells just where the waves washed in. Dry in the sand, the stones were silent as old bones, but wet, they told stories. Wet, they gave up their secrets, exposing their memories of skeletal fragments, delicate traces of extinct crustaceans and prehistoric ferns. My father told me all this and showed me how to see the stones in the world around me and how to see the world in the stones. Every time I found one I called out, "Fossil!" and by naming them possessed them, made them mine.

Of course, I kept as many as I could, collecting them every time we went to the lake and putting the best ones in a six-quart basket in the back of the old Plymouth to take home to Elmira, the small town where we lived a few hours inland. I stored them in the basement behind the furnace, occasionally going down to feel them, to finger the curve of some embedded creature or the fluted grooves of a leaf. Down there in the dim cellar I would often feel inexplicably sad, perhaps because only wet did the stones and pebbles glow, and these in the basket were lifeless unless I spat on them. Here was my first lesson in emotional archeology: the importance of context and the problem of removal from site. Or perhaps the sadness arose because, although I loved collecting these stones, I really didn't have any idea what to *do* with them. I simply needed to have them and to hold them in my hands.

The rocks in the cellar were discarded decades ago, but I still collect stones and shells, for it seems I am not myself unless I have a few pieces of the planet close at hand. They are needed as reminders, as mnemonic objects that, in their own mute way, prompt me to look for stories and then to tell them. Stones are cues, leading me back and forth in time until I am here, putting words on the page.

Like fossils set in limestone, words impress themselves on paper, syllables shrinking history into a legible construct. Real fossils are time's shorthand, abbreviated geology: anonymous footprints in the mud are eternally available once they are uncovered. Sometimes the long-dead thing and the stone are one, like the small trilobite lying still as if asleep in the museum case, silent and precise. Fossils, like books, constrict the world into compact, containable things you can hold in your hand or carry around in your pocket.

Since childhood when I first began to understand what words can do, I have wanted to make, out of the life around me, something else that will endure when I am gone. Just as fossils tell only part of the story, my stories are only partial truths—but insofar as they exist, they change life into language and keep it firm. From an Egyptian box inlaid with three kinds of wood I take out a winkle shell picked up at the Butt of Lewis, a sharp wedge of gleaming black obsidian taken from an island in Lake Naivasha, a spiral of coral lifted from a Cuban beach, and a handful of other sweet and shapely stones and shells whose origins are now obscure but whose existence seems essential to my well-being.

Here's a small lump of chalky rock I took from the path ten years ago as we hiked up to a hilltop shrine dedicated to poor old Saint Sebastian, his slender plaster body shedding paint and all pierced through with arrows. The sky was silky-grey that day, and the wind was fierce, the way it often is up in the high hills of Languedoc in the south of France. The air smelled of wild thyme, and from the shrine one could look out far, far out over mountainous ridges falling away blue in the distance like the closing chords of a great hymn. Languedoc, where the blood of heretics, Cathar or Calvinist, was spilled for hundreds of years by Roman Catholic armies from the north, where that blood leached into the stony soil and vanished—but for the awful stories of belief adamant in the face of death. There are no fossils to tell these tales: instead, what remains are ruined castles and broken walls, and these small shrines belonging to the victors. Stones piled upon stones, and stories wherever there are stones.

Around the time I was so enamoured of fossils, an adult friend of the family gave me a small chunk of iron pyrite. *Fool's gold,* he said. I am holding it now, and it sits like a dense and brassy toad in my palm, catching the light—but it doesn't shine like real gold: there's a kind of nasty, greenish tone. Even if you weren't a trained prospector, you'd know this wasn't genuine. Still, holding this thing in one hand, then the other, I find myself wondering if I might not, some-times, be taken for a fool by all that glitters. But it is real, this false thing. It is real iron pyrite. I am incapable of throwing it out, although I've had it for more than fifty years, hating it all that while. I shove it firmly in closed boxes or hide it at the back of drawers, and still it finds its way out now and again, emerging triumphant. And every time I say, "Oh, heaven help us, there's that damn fool's gold again."

Something happens to the objects we keep, even those we do not love. They acquire a patina of legitimacy, a dignity sprung from longevity making it unthinkably rude to toss them aside. Besides, I know that if I were to cast this pyrite out, it would hunch down glowering in the garbage, beaming powerful signals in the manner of some comic-book cosmic element until I dutifully retrieved it and put it back in my life. What does the fool's gold *mean?* Well, I suppose once I know *that,* then it will allow itself to be lost. There is some lesson for me in this silly hunk of metal. And as long as I need the lesson, I must keep the thing.

Stones, shells, muddled memorabilia clutter surfaces wherever I make my home. My desk is crowded with china bowls, enamelled tins, small wooden boxes and sweet-grass baskets, old crockery packed with coloured glass and calling cards: how can I justify this mess? In his essay "The Morality of Things," Bruce Chatwin wrote that "things have a way of insinuating themselves into all human lives. Some people attract more things than others, but no people, however mobile, is *thingless.* A chimpanzee uses sticks and stones as tools, but he does not keep possessions. Man does. And the things to which he becomes most attached do not serve any useful function. Instead they are symbols, or emotional anchors. The question I should like to ask (without necessarily being able to answer it) is, 'Why are man's real treasures useless?'"

What a shame that Bruce is dead, for I would answer his question with another: who is to say what "use" is? I find these things around me useful—the intricate engines of memory, as powerful as machines. The stone appears to be a stone, but within itself there is a throbbing energy: it is not an anchor but a ship.

On a shelf above my desk there sits the small glass bird my husband gave me when our baby was born, a plastic Virgin half-full of holy water from Lourdes, a film canister packed with blood-red soil from Kenya, a silver-rimmed maté cup from Argentina, a small wooden Buddha, and a round, birch-bark basket decorated with porcupine quills I bought on Manitoulin Island, at the top of Lake Huron, the summer I was nineteen and in love with a man who was fired from the American-owned lodge where we both worked because he was seen holding my hand. Because I was white and he was Ojibwa. My first encounter with prejudice and injustice but, for him, only one of many. The colours of the quills have faded over forty years, but I look at that basket and see his face, and hear his soft voice, and remember the way he showed me how to hold a paddle for the J-stroke.

I need these odds and ends around me. They are my comfort, my solace, my way of establishing *place* no matter where I happen to be living. With baskets of stones and shells I carry with me not only memory but emotional furnishings. I have never written the story of this man whose name was George, but I have written, and will continue to write, about love and loss and confusion.

Since my earliest days I have been a merchant for Nostalgia, setting up my souvenir stall on the road to the wharf on the River Styx. I do not hoard memories and I am willing—even eager—to part with them.

"Here now, sir, here's something to take in the boat with you as you pass on to the other side. A line of poetry smooth as a pebble, a phrase bright as an insect's wing, a clause transparent as snakeskin shed in the grass. Take these souvenirs, if you wish, you who travel forward, and keep them close to your heart as you move into the darkness. You cannot take your gold and jewels, you cannot take your fossils. But you can take your stories across the water."

The following objects exist in a small blue bag I carry
with me when I travel. They may also exist in the mind
of the goddess who determines where and how stories
are born: a dried scarlet runner bean, a small penknife,
a shard of Cretan pottery, two baby teeth, and this key
chain attached to a small music box which tinkles the
first bars of "Für Elise." My father bought it in Beijing
for my mother the year before she died. And a polished
oval of sodalite, blue as lapis lazuli, placed in my hand
long ago by a professor of philosophy I loved until he
died. Still love, still visit in my dreams. My philoso-
pher's stone. My stories.

Here, look at this. These pearl buttons I keep in this
stoneware jar, just large enough to hold all twelve.
They're from my mother's uniform when she was a
nurse, during the Depression. They're mother-of-
pearl—see how they're attached to these small metal
hooks? You slide them through two buttonholes at
once and then you twist and they won't ever come
undone.

Let the buttons slip through your fingers now, all
twelve, and contemplate the starched white cotton

bodices and cuffs these pearl-faced clasps were meant to close. Consider the nurses' lives so carefully fastened too, the way they dressed so much a part of how they behaved as women. Think about my mother, who worried throughout her life about her too-exuberant laugh. "My awful horse laugh," she called it. Lips unbuttoned and mouth wide open—unfeminine, she was told. A woman should not toss her head back when she laughs. A lady should never show her molars.

Pick up the stoneware jar, with its pretty lid of crackled green glass, and you will never guess what it contains, nor that the thing itself was a farewell gift from a woman with whom I have been friends since we met in Toronto in our first jobs after university. We went off to England in 1966 and shared a bed-sitter in Earls' Court; London spread itself before us like a magic feast we could devour forever and never be full. I hear Sheila's voice when I look at the jar, saying goodbye as she gave it to me the day I before I left for home because my mother was ill.

If I lift the glass lid, my mother's voice comes out so loud and clear that Sheila's dies away and disappears. Only my mother's is left, telling me stories about how she loved nursing and expressing her ardent hope that I too one day would take up this honest work. "Oh you'd be such a good nurse, darling," she'd say. "You have the hands for it, you'd be so good." But I did not want to be good. I wanted to be a writer.

The jar is open now, and the old-fashioned buttons are emptied out: useless things of shell and steel. My mother's laugh was so big and wonderful that she seemed sometimes in danger of surrendering to her own delight, and all her life it embarrassed her. Her natural capacity for joy made her feel ashamed.

My mother's laughing is part of the fossil of my life, and I can't understand what it means, not yet anyway. And so I write about it, and the other memories that haunt me, until I do. The lid is off. The buttons are out and talking, telling me truths, stating the obvious. I would have been a good nurse. The older I get, the more I suspect my mother was right, I should have been a nurse. These strong, long-fingered hands of mine tapping the keys could be stroking a forehead or soothing a brow. Doing some good. Instead, I nurse words and coax stories to life. What good is that?

I haven't sprung from the oral tradition. I have no family lineage in which there sang a troubadour, I don't sing folk ballads while strumming the guitar. Singing stories has to do with plot, who did what to whom and why, and then the chorus again to make sure we remember and get it right. I belong to the other tribe, who painted dreams on the walls of caves, who stacked up stones on the tops of hills, who left behind *things* to mark their passing and to make you remember in your own way. I am one of them, putting things into words. My basket of stones. My mother's buttons. Things turning into words turning into things again: stone, word, book.

GRACELAND

Ottawa, 1987

AIR SHARP AND COLD AS STEEL against my cheeks, cold and sharp as my blades cutting into the ice, I speed round the curves of the oval rink, my body bent forward and my arms swinging from side to side. Looking up, once the wind's at my back, I notice one last star fading as dawn opens out across the snow-covered spaces of Brewer's Park. I am skating like fury, skating my heart out, skating to beat back the bad dreams and to start the day fresh and fearless. I love the way these February mornings come up pale, the colour of thinned-out lemonade. I love the sensation of my face being polished by the wind and my legs being stretched and warmed by exertion. I love being alone, skating around the oval.

My dreams are of Africa, where I've never been and where I am going. Awake, I am brave and excited, but in my sleep, I cry out in alarm. In only a few months I will be in Kenya, trying to remember what it's like to be this cold. My husband, Bob, has taken a job in Nairobi, having been assured it's for only two years. He'll be setting up a new communications division for a research centre funded by the international development organization for which he works. We tell ten-year-old Abbey that this will be an exciting adventure for her, and after it's over we'll come back to this city where we've made our home for the past seven years, where we have established our careers and anchored ourselves in the comfortable neighbourhood of Ottawa South. We tell ourselves that going abroad will open us up to the world and open up the world to us.

Still, I am loath to leave behind all that is dear and familiar, and to give up my place at the university where I teach creative writing. I must work hard to believe that leaving is part of my destiny too, I must skate myself into the space that fate decrees. There is no point in swimming against the tide, I admonish myself as I skate. I must let myself slide into the future, see what it has to offer, stop putting up barriers to new experience. Skating my psyche into submission, I glide, the long fine stride of my body and my out-flung arms making an outward show of joy. The little foam pads of a Walkman fit against my ears under my rabbit-fur hat and fill my head with the sounds of Africa. I am skating to *Graceland*, Paul Simon and Ladysmith Black Mambazo heating up my brain: the clever lyrics are New York hip, but it's not the words, it's the music that pulls me forward around the ice, the rhythm of the drumming, those deep dark voices, chanting and calling out. Taking me to live under African skies.

I am in the kitchen, on the telephone with my friend Sally, a perfectly intelligent woman I've known since childhood. She teaches mathematics in a suburb of Toronto, and we don't see each other much anymore; nevertheless, we still feel as if we are related—cousins, maybe—having grown up in Elmira, Ontario, where our parents played bridge together once a month for nearly thirty years. I have called to tell Sally that I am leaving the country in a few months' time, and she says, I feel stupid asking this, but where exactly *is* Nairobi, and I say, well, can you see the map of Africa in your mind's eye, and she says yes, and I say, okay then, can you sort of see where Egypt is, at the top right-hand corner? Yes? And see the Nile delta? Then go down the Nile and about halfway, on the right-hand side of the map, that's Kenya, and . . .

Here, I notice my husband, who is in the kitchen with me, motioning me with his finger raised as if he has something essential he needs to tell me. Yes, Bob, what? I say, a little annoyed that he's interrupting. He says, pointing, it's up the Nile. You go *up* a river to its source, which in this case is Lake Victoria. He is smiling, being helpful.

Oh Jesus in heaven, I say, she knows what I mean. Don't you, Sally? And of course she does, she's followed my impeccable directions because we see things the same way, we inhabited the same classrooms where the Cadbury World always hung at one side of the blackboard. We come from the same rolling green corner of Ontario, from where the rest of the world looked flat as a map and, if it existed at all, was coloured in pastel chunks. Kenya was pink like England, like Canada, like all the other countries of the Empire in which we were meant to believe. And you would find it there, on the right-hand side of Africa, at the bottom of the Nile. I realize, talking to Sally, that I have no *real* idea where I'm going.

Bob knows, however. He's already been to Kenya several times, the first when he was a lad of eighteen doing his British National Service in the Royal Air Force, an experience of such positive contrast to his boyhood in Edinburgh that he has ever since felt an affinity to the country and its people. That early exposure to Africa altered the choices he made in the years that followed and changed the direction of his life— but neither of us suspects how changing countries, even temporarily, is going to change *us*. He hopes that this job will open doors for him in the future, but we do not yet know the windows and doors in our hearts that will be opened—be wrenched open and torn from their hinges, never to be shut again. We do not know that we have begun a long journey with no return.

When we get to Nairobi in late July, it is not at all what I have imagined. African skies turn out to be the dull, heavy colour of iron. The rainy season has begun and the wind is cold and mean, the air smells like diesel and sewers, the sidewalks near the hotel are broken and dirty and weeds flourish in the cracks. Everything I look at seems ugly except for a cascade of pink bougainvillea by the hotel pool and the yellow blossoms of oleander trees along the avenues. But in this context the beauty of flowers seems inane, a kind of futile camouflage, a bright smile trying, and failing, to disguise pain.

We have great difficulty in finding a house to rent and must remain in the hotel for several weeks. However, Ballou, our little grey cat, arrives on schedule, shipped in his travelling cage from a kennel outside Ottawa where he stayed while we stopped in France to see friends en route. We have had Ballou for only three years, but he has become such a part of our family that we never considered leaving him behind. He joins us now in the room, disoriented and stressed, cowering beneath the beds and making high, sorrowful screeches when we try to pull him out.

We accustom ourselves to the oddities of hotel life: maid service, room service, waiters in the dining room taking our order, leaning down and smiling big smiles to rhyme off their fresh juices: "Passion?" We get to know the staff at the reception desk by name as we sit in the lobby and watch the tourists come and go, obvious and awkward in their pockety vests and Tilley hats. We chat with the doormen, who advise us to be watchful of thieves on the streets, telling us each time we go out as if it is new information. We notice the same beautiful African girls at the entrance to the bar every day, and I explain to Abbey what they do for a living, and we talk about AIDS. We go to the kitchen to ask for scraps for Ballou, who has lost his appetite, and come away with a fine dish of steamed scallops the cook says he hopes will "make kitty happy." I eat a few in the elevator on the way to our room and, indeed, feel happier myself.

We are invited to a party being hosted by a young doctor from Toronto whose field is AIDS and whose research involves those same young women we've seen in the bar. Many other expatriates have been invited, and his apartment is full to overflowing: everyone but me seems to be involved in some variety of meaningful aid work. We sit on the floor and eat macadamia nuts and drink Tusker beer and make conversation. A rosy-cheeked and animated Englishwoman tells me about her breast-feeding education program. She and her team are teaching Kenyan mothers to ignore the bright and appealing ads for dried milk formula, slowly convincing them to breast-feed their babies again, to go back to traditional ways rather than turn to the modern.

It all seems crazily backward, how first we come and undo their lives and then we come and undo them again, we foreign experts who seem to know everything and who, without meaning to, divide the world into *them* and *us*. Can nobody get it right? Should we be here at all? The room seems, suddenly, filled with oppressive good intent, and I feel lost and overfull of macadamias. The host keeps the music turned up loudly and everyone seems to be shouting, and I am thinking I need to go home. But just at this moment someone flicks in a tape of *Graceland*, and all at once I am skating into the wind again, down in Brewer's Park in the morning. In my head I fling myself backward against the current of time and glide away from the hot noisy room and feel the snow blowing like small sharp diamonds on my face. Saved! And by little Paul Simon at that.

Finally, in mid-September, we move into a large white stucco house on a residential road that was once a coffee estate, high up on the northern flank of the city where the air is clean and the nights are cool. The contrast between this tranquil green landscape and the polluted centre of Nairobi is so vivid that we are disoriented until we accustom ourselves to the sound of birds and monkeys instead of traffic, the smell of frangipani and roses instead of smoke and garbage. The lawns around the house are shaded by flowering trees—bombax and nandi flame, grevillea, cassia, jacaranda—and in the garden stands an avocado tree, laden with ripe fruit. We tell ourselves and Ballou, who is mesmerized by the darting lizards and flickering sunbirds, that we have died and gone to heaven. I wonder what I was so afraid of, back in Ottawa, during those weeks of nightmares.

In fact, I am not fearful at all, although a bit fazed by the social necessity of having house staff. We hire a pretty and well-spoken Kikuyu woman named Mary to help with cooking and cleaning, and retain the services of a gardener who has already been employed on this property. His name is Benson and, like many other gardeners on this road, he is Abaluya from Kakamega near Lake Victoria. A sweet-natured man in his late thirties, he shouts and claps his hands in glee when he sees that we have brought with us a power lawn mower from Canada, for until now he has used a scythe the way most gardeners do.

We are his first Canadians, and Mary's too. They both take delight in instructing us how to avoid perils in this unfamiliar setting. Benson insists that all snakes are poisonous and must be killed on sight, and perhaps for that reason we never see snakes in the garden—if they're around, they keep a low profile. We follow Mary's careful kitchen rules, and take precautions by boiling our drinking water and the raw milk we get from a cow down the road. She scrubs all vegetables and fruit bought in the market with a stiff brush but agrees that using chlorine beach, as some nervous foreigners do, is not necessary. We take our malaria tablets if we leave the city, we shake our shirts and sheets coming off the clothesline to rid them of insects, we check Ballou and our new dogs—two golden labradors, an old fellow already called Teddy and a female pup we name Alice—for ticks. We lock our doors and windows and, every night, we close the protective metal grille at the top of the stairs between the bedrooms and the rest of the house. We are sensible, we are prudent. We never wear gold jewellery or carry cash when we go down into the city, but we always make sure we have coins to give the parking boys because if we don't our tires will be slashed. Or so we are told.

I also give coins to the old beggars who make their rounds on Biashara Street, where Asian merchants in the dry-goods shops ensure their days in Paradise with Sabbath almsgiving. Some of them keep a brass plate full of coins by their front door on Fridays, and the beggars simply help themselves—nip in the door, palm a few shillings and shuffle on out again, their presence essential to the spiritual well-being of the prosperous

Muslim businessmen. As I am in the process of setting up our house, I spend a good deal of time on Biashara choosing curtains and cushions: it is here that I begin to see how things fit together differently from anything I've known before. The idea that the businessmen might need the beggars? A revelation. What else might there be to learn?

Outside the coffee house on Kenyatta Avenue where I buy bags of freshly roasted beans, there is usually a woman sitting on the pavement. It is not always the same one, although I would be hard-pressed to distinguish among them, these thin women dressed in rags holding snuffling, lethargic babies on their laps. She always sits with her bare feet stuck straight out, legs like two brown sticks beneath the cotton *kanga*. The tin cup is either beside her or between her calloused feet. As she raises her eyes to mine, she makes little moaning noises low in her throat. I hate the way she looks at me and I hate the way I am looking back at her. Whether I give her money or not, it is never enough. It can never make a difference; she will be there again tomorrow, beseeching, unless I take her home, and what then? I leave with her eyes hot on my retreating back and feel her angry despair drilling into me for hours after. There is no doubt in my mind that this woman— every one of them—hates me, no matter how many coins I make clatter into her small cup. Now I am on the edge of understanding, and the accompanying sense of culpability—although I've been told to expect it, I've been warned that this is part of the "overseas posting package"—is excruciating.

While we live in Kenya, I say, I want to know Kenyans, not foreigners like myself. It is possibly a noble senti-ment, but also rather stupid and self-limiting. Nevertheless, I refuse to join expatriate clubs and organizations—such as the entirely worthy Museum Society—and decide to make my own way into the African world around me. Easier said than done, of course, for my status as "spouse" makes it nearly impossible to work (unless I take a teaching job at the American School, which I do not want to do), and I am lonely for a long time. However, despite myself, I become friends with other foreigners, and eventually I find several Kenyan friends from various walks of life—and the very first is Rachel.

Rachel lives in a small mud-walled house in a cluster of similar dwellings along a narrow dirt track about two kilometres from where I live in our eight-room house surrounded by tended lawns and gardens. She is just a few years younger than me, forty years old, separated from her husband (a polite way of saying that he has gone off and left her), and mother of three children. She cares for her elderly parents, her father nearly blind and her mother too feeble to do much else but spend her days sitting on a bench outside the house. Rachel's income is from her job as a domestic in Nairobi, work she has been doing for foreign families for half her life.

Which is how I meet her. I am the final link in a transfer of money to Rachel from a former English employer who has moved back to London and who sends occasional cheques to her via another Englishwoman in Nairobi named Ruth, whom I meet after Abbey begins attending the same small British school as her children do. Ruth cashes these cheques for pounds sterling into Kenyan shillings and gives the money to me in the school parking lot. I then take the gift home for Rachel, who can more conveniently collect it at my house than at Ruth's across the city.

As soon as I see her, the day she first comes for her money, I like Rachel. For a start, we are both tall and stand eye to eye. She does not speak in a servile way, nor does she call me *memsahib*, but looks at me straight on, woman to woman, no false humility in her acceptance of the money she needs. She is wearing the garb of service, a pink-and-white-checked cotton dress with white collar and cuffs, and a white scarf tied in a knot at the back of her head, but her dignified manner makes the uniform invisible.

By the second occasion we meet, enough time has passed that I am more comfortable in my skin here, and I invite her into the house where we stand chatting

easily about our mutual acquaintance Ruth, and her
friend the Englishwoman who sends the money. Rachel
tells me about her children, particularly the problem
she's having with Lois, her eldest who is "running
wild." As she is leaving, she thanks me, and in doing so,
calls me Isabel. I don't suggest she should not, although
I know it is not conventional etiquette. But this unspeak-
able boldness and breaking of social rules enrages
Mary, who is down the hall listening. She tells me that
Rachel is a bad woman, and I understand immediately
that she is jealous. When Rachel appears the next time at
the door asking to speak to Isabel, Mary calls out,
"Missus, you have some visitor here," in a tight, angry
voice. She refuses to speak to Rachel and walks off into
the kitchen where she bangs things noisily.

They are both Kikuyu women of similar age, but
they differ in appearance: Mary is small and slim and
fine-featured, and Rachel is large, a hearty woman with
round hips and a wide, generous smile. She's intelligent and literate, as is Mary, both of them far too smart
to be doing the menial work they do, but both locked
by circumstance into the low social level of housework
and childcare that, ironically, pays more and gives better benefits than most jobs they could get in Nairobi. It
is Mary who tells me this, explaining that although she
has enough education to work in an office or a shop,
she'd be able to save nothing, as every penny would go
for clothes, transportation, housing, food.

In fact, Mary is particularly enterprising and during her years of service has accumulated enough money to buy plots of land around the city, in squatter areas and in the slums of Kariobangi. There, she has built shacks in which she rents out rooms: with this money she buys more land in her home village near Nyeri, land that will someday belong to her three sons. She takes me to see some of her newly built rental units, warning me beforehand that I will be seeing "very poor people"— but still I am unprepared for the filth and squalor. As we make our way under corrugated iron roofs hanging over the muddy walkways between shacks, I must constantly duck my head—which throws me off balance, so that I lose my footing and step into an open sewer running down the centre of the path. It is clear from the way Mary watches as I clean the smelly gunk off my leg that she enjoys providing this lesson in urban reality. I am distressed by the poverty and appalled by the stench but, in the end, amused and intrigued by Mary herself. My housekeeper, slum landlord.

Mary takes a deep dislike to Rachel and warns me against her, saying that she is "too tricky." I laugh, because common gossip is that *all* Kikuyu people are clever, wily and not to be trusted, but when I tease Mary about this, she sniffs and mutters, "You see. You wait." Sure enough, one afternoon when she arrives at the house, our dog Teddy jumps up on Rachel and frightens her, and by the time I get to the door she is wailing and wringing her hands. Her dress is slightly ripped, and she says the dog has bitten her breast, she is in pain and we must do something, we must take care of her. Mary is indignant and takes me aside, warning me that it is all an act, a ruse to get money out of us. "That dog Teddy never did bite her," she says. "He too old."

Rachel will not let me see her breast but applies a cold wet washcloth to it herself. When she is calm, I give her the envelope of cash and she leaves. We wait, but she never takes the matter further; she never goes for a doctor's certificate to prove that she's been bitten (the way that cunning Mary would have done) and that she needs financial help for medical expenses. She has simply established that we have *nearly* been responsible for harm *nearly* done her. Somehow, by this act she makes clear that we are connected at another, deeper level.

Months pass, and I visit Rachel at her house when there's another small parcel of money to hand over, because that's easier than antagonizing Mary or risking another episode with the dog. It takes less than half an hour to walk from my place to hers, but in the process I leave one world and enter another. On Lone Tree Estate, where I live, the houses are set well back from the road, protected by three-metre-high hedges and solid metal gates, usually closed and manned by one of the gardeners or a uniformed guard from a security company. We leave our gate open on the advice of Benson, who says that gangs of thieves will come whether or not the gate is closed. Open, it gives the agreeable impression that we are not rich and have nothing to steal—and besides, it is less work for Benson, since our property is large and running to open the gate is wearisome. He appears to be right, as we are never robbed, although we often hear that others along our road are. The houses are owned by wealthy black, white and Asian Kenyans, and some are rented to foreigners like us—but we meet very few neighbours, because there is no common ground where we might see each other.

However, as I walk along the road, I am never alone. There are out-of-work men lounging and smoking on the grassy verge by the hedges, and knots of uniformed house-girls clustered together under scarlet poinsettia and hibiscus, exchanging news and laughter. Everyone greets me as they greet each other: "*Jambo! Habari yako?*" To which one replies, "*Mẓuri sana. Na wewe?*" (Hi there, how are you? Fine, thanks. And you?) These routine phrases traded back and forth are the first I learn, and I like the chance to speak Swahili, a language easy to pronounce and satisfying in the mouth.

About half a kilometre from my house, the road splits off into two narrow tracks. One weaves down through tall grass and colourful lantana bushes into a valley of dense bush where beehives hang from branches, humming in the wild green heat. The other path passes through a corridor of cedar until finally it comes out and streaks straight as an arrow through fields of coffee bordered by small houses and gardens—*shambas* of maize and yams and black-eyed beans and potatoes. The houses vary in size, from the substantial cement-brick bungalows of the prosperous to the small mud-wall dwellings of the less fortunate, all with rusting metal roofs and dusty front yards in which chickens flutter and peck in the red dirt and skinny goats wander around with the dogs, aimless and bored.

Rachel's house sits behind a low wooden fence painted blue, which is how I am able to identify it the first time, according to her instructions. Nevertheless, I frequently stop and ask where she lives— *"Wapi nyumba Rachel?"*—so that everyone will know I have a specific reason to be there: it is clear that my presence is out of the ordinary, for children gawk and giggle and some of the adult stares are less than friendly. Rachel's house is about the size of a two-car garage, with a hard-packed dirt floor swept so clean that it is nearly like clay tile. I stand at the open door and look in: a low-wattage bulb hanging from the ceiling casts a sad grey light. The main room is painted sea green and decorated with calendars and framed photographs hung high on the walls, and there are two matching armchairs and a chesterfield, covered in shiny brown vinyl, exactly like the sets we bought for both Mary and Benson, who have their own separate living quarters on our property, and with the same kind of crocheted doilies over their backs and arms. A little girl in a dirty red dress squints at me from a corner and tells me in a sullen voice that her mother is not home.

I turn back and try to speak with Rachel's small, wrinkled mother, who is seated on the bench, stringing beans, but as she speaks only Kikuyu, my offerings of Swahili are worthless. The old lady's clothes are clean, but ragged beyond belief. Her husband sits on a stool beneath a guava tree nearby, and when I go over to introduce myself and shake his hand, his clouded old eyes cannot see me, but his face lights up with a smile, and we exchange a few words. Another of Rachel's children appears, a boy who seems a little older than the girl and who is certainly more friendly. His name is Ronnie, and he is a chatterbox. He shows me around and takes me through their *shamba*, a green jumble of kale and onions and peas shaded by a large stand of bananas. He introduces me to a cow named Milcah grazing in their yard: she belongs to a neighbour who allows Rachel to have the milk. But his mother sells it six days out of seven, says Ronnie, because they need the money. The family drinks milk only on Sundays.

Ronnie tells me his sister Grace is eight and he will soon be ten, and puts out his hand to shake mine when I leave. "You are my mother's good friend," he says, and I worry that he might think it is from me that the gifts of money come, but I don't know how to clear up the misunderstanding. On the path I meet Rachel, who is stricken that she has not been there to give me tea. It is a terrible shame, she says, that I was not received properly. I promise to return in a day or two, but we decide to transfer the money right then from my pocket to hers, being extremely careful not to be observed making the transaction. For me to be seen carrying shillings to Rachel would put us both at risk: in a society as poor as this one, robbery exists as a constant possibility, and only the rich and foolish would allow themselves to be seen with cash in hand.

I go for tea later that week, and soon fall into the habit of walking to Rachel's every few days, becoming a familiar enough figure so that children no longer point and giggle. Instead, there are nods of recognition that I am not just a white stranger, I am Rachel's friend, her Canadian *rafiki*. Some days I hike past Rachel's house out into the rolling green hills of the tea estates, simply for the pleasure of being in open country under a cloudless dome of African blue. I am deeply happy in this landscape. Finally, after many months, I am grateful to Bob for bringing us to Africa.

Slowly, I get to know Rachel, sitting with her and talking over tea. Most of our conversations concern her failing parents or her headstrong and defiant daughter Lois, who, at eighteen, has already had one baby out of wedlock. Rachel, an ardent Christian, prays for guidance in this matter, but it seems that God does not hear, for Lois looks thick around the middle, as if she might be pregnant again. And we talk about young Grace, who appears to have a learning disability and must have special schooling. In this context my own problems wane in importance, for I cannot help comparing Rachel's life and mine, the result of which makes me feel ashamed that I have ever complained.

Sometimes Rachel asks for a loan, just until the next gift of money comes from the Englishwoman, and I most often say that she need not pay it back as the amounts are small. But I swear her to secrecy because there'd be a terrible ruckus if Mary ever found out. She has warned me over and over, "That Rachel, she only like you because you rich. She try to use you."

But I am using Rachel, it seems to me. She has opened a door into a place I would never have gone without her.

As we enter the second year of our friendship, Rachel is able to ask for many things besides money, in return for which she gives me small sweet bananas from her garden. She asks if I will drive Grace to her special school each day as it is near Abbey's school bus stop, and I agree without hesitation. One day she asks if I could make a birthday cake for Ronnie, as she doesn't have an oven and her employer in Nairobi has forbidden her to make food for herself in that kitchen. I use an angel food cake mix I brought from Canada, and I decorate it with thick icing in different colours. I buy candles and balloons so that Rachel can give him a proper party, and I give Ronnie some paper and coloured pencils. It is the best birthday he's ever had, he says, and his eyes are sparkling as he hugs me.

Mary is stony-faced with anger when she catches me icing the cake and refuses to speak to me for several days. When she learns, a few weeks later, that Rachel has asked me to go to her church for a Mothers' Union service, she laughs derisively and says I'd better take a lot of money, because that's why I've been invited: to make a large donation at the *harambee* following the service. "You be the only white person there, and you be expected to give many hundred shillings, I warn you."

I am, as she predicted, the only *mʒungu* in the crowded church. Since I know many of the evangelical hymns from my childhood summers at church camp, I join in with zeal, although I am the only one singing in English. The service is in Kikuyu, and I understand nothing except the welcome that is given me from the pulpit.

Then comes the *harambee*, a fund-raising system beloved in Kenya, when large sums of money must be drawn from the populace. I know the term means "self-help," and I read in the newspapers every day about *harambees* being held for various reasons—to help a family, build a school, finance a political party—but this is my first direct experience. At first, individuals get up and walk to the front of the church to put money in the basket, where a team of men and women are standing, waiting to receive each person with a handshake. With every donation, a man announces the name of the giver and the amount given, and the congregation claps enthusiastically. I listen to the amounts and decide that one hundred shillings sounds about right. I am pink-faced with embarrassment when I finally go up and put the bill in the basket. My name is called out and I am applauded.

I think, There now, that's over—not understanding *harambee*. This, it turns out, is only the warm-up. After some wonderfully harmonious singing by the Fathers' Union, a basket is passed along the rows, and people continue to put money in. Then again, individuals to the front of the church, names called, applause. This goes on many times—five, six, seven—like squeezing an orange to get every last sweet drop of juice. Everyone is in high spirits, and the total is tallied after each donation session, and another brief speech is made by one of the team standing at the front of the church, exhorting us to give more. We've only just begun.

I bless Mary's name for having prepared me so that I have brought enough cash and wonder why Rachel didn't forewarn me. Had she thought I'd know? Or did she think I might not come if she explained what the service would entail?

When there's not a penny left in any purse, the team is satisfied, and we all go outside where tables are set up for a feast brought by the women of the congregation. I am urged to eat everything—roasted goat and beef stew and maize and *sukama weki* and *irio*—by Rachel's friends, who must see me tucking into their dishes in order to verify that I am truly glad to be there. I eat the food with many exclamations of appreciation, and wash it all down with orange Fanta, and then I make my rounds, shaking hands and congratulating the women on such a fine meal. Rachel is beaming, she wants me to be having a good time. And I am. When we drive away from the church at the end of the afternoon, she reaches over and strokes my arm and I press her hand with mine. We are both of us pleased with ourselves.

Toward the end of our second year, it becomes apparent that Bob must stay for a third in order to accomplish the work he has come to do. Strangely, this change of plans is exhilarating rather than upsetting: both

Abbey and I have come to love Kenya nearly as much as he does and are as happy as he is that the contract has been extended. When we tell Benson and Mary that we can employ them for another year, they too are elated, although each is hoping that the other will depart. They are frequently not on speaking terms, communicating their dislike with much slamming of the kitchen door that opens to the garden and dog kennels. No matter that we believe we are completely even-handed, there exists between them a growing rivalry for our affection and for benefits that might accrue from being favoured.

During our summer leave in Ottawa, we tell our friends and neighbours we will be home soon, but secretly we are eager to get back to Kenya and to make the most of our final ten months. It has taken us two years to adjust, and now we feel we are ready to *live*. When we return to Nairobi in August, we receive an affectionate and noisy welcome from Teddy and Alice as soon as we get out of the car, and Ballou weaves himself happily around our legs in greeting. Indoors, Mary has set bouquets of lilies and jasmine around the living room, and Benson has laid big logs of gumwood for a fire. We have brought them presents from Canada, and there is a festive air as the five of us share a meal of roast chicken and *ugali*, the thick maize porridge we now like better than mashed potatoes.

My initial cynicism about foreign involvement in this country has diminished over time, partly because I have learned how great the need is for help of any kind—and not only for the living but for the dying. I learn about the latter from Ruth, the woman to whom Rachel's money is sent from England, and with whom I have become friends—we have branched out now from conversations in the parking lot to afternoon teas to family dinners. Ruth is a nurse whose volunteer work in the slums has convinced her of the urgent need for a hospice. With extraordinary energy and spirit, she begins campaigns in Kenya and England to get funds and government assistance to achieve this goal.

The hospice will be for cancer patients, but unspoken is the fact that some system of caregiving is going to be needed in future for the increasing number of AIDS cases. Ruth's proposal consists of an outreach program that will radiate throughout Nairobi from a small centre situated near Kenyatta Hospital. It will be staffed by Kenyan nurses and expatriate volunteers who will go into the homes of the dying not only to administer medication but to give support and instruction to the families as well. Ruth's efforts pay off, and the hospice is built and opened in February 1990. I attend the first training sessions for caregivers and am eager to go out in a nursing capacity, but as I will soon be leaving the country it is decided that my energies will be put to better use producing the hospice newsletter.

I spend many hours at the hospice in order to get material for newsletter stories. The Kenyan nurses are the kind of women I admire: dedicated, strong and endlessly cheerful. I become friends with several and with the director, Bridgid, in particular. Like Rachel, she is a tall woman, extremely direct and open, one of those exceptional people who manage to be efficient and relaxed at the same time. Every time we meet, it seems that our conversation is spiced with laughter; Bridgid always has funny stories to relate. I learn at the hospice that humour is an essential component in the care of the dying, for although laughter cannot eradicate pain, it is an analgesic for the spirit.

However, when the time comes for us to leave Kenya, I am far too sad to make jokes. The day I turn up at her office to say goodbye, my face streaked with tears, Bridgid holds me in a long embrace to comfort me and to assure me that she understands my distress. Having finally discovered a way to be useful, I find it hard to leave.

By the time we depart Nairobi in the summer, Mary has already left us. Increasingly jealous of Benson, she tells a series of compelling and intricate lies in an attempt get him fired, but they have the unhappy effect of exposing her duplicity, and in the end we have no choice but to "let her go." We hire no one else: Benson sometimes helps with the housework and I help him in the garden. The place feels happier and lighter without Mary's moody, rancorous presence, but I miss her and regret the angry and bitter way our relationship ended.

I am seeing Rachel less often now: for one thing, the Englishwoman has stopped sending money. I still drive Grace to her school in the mornings, and I walk down the path to visit from time to time, but I worry that Rachel is hoping I will take over the role of benefactor and we have already committed ourselves to Benson. Since visiting his Kakamega village and meeting his wife, Jane, and the children, we've decided to continue helping with their school fees after we leave. Although in theory education in Kenya is freely available, in reality the system is honeycombed with hidden expenses, making it all but impossible for rural families to keep children in school. Sending money to Benson, through his next employer on this Lone Tree Estate property, seems an easy enough thing to do.

But at the last minute our plans change and we do not go home. Bob is told that his former position in Ottawa is guaranteed for only one year after his return: it seems likely that he will have to look for a new job and, at fifty-eight, he considers that a daunting prospect. Coincidentally, at this very moment he is offered a three-year contract for similar work at an international development centre in Montpellier, a city in the south of France famous for scientific research. For two weeks we do little but make lists of advantages and disadvantages, which turn out to be the same length every time. In the end, we are swayed by meeting a French family on the train when we go to the coast for Abbey's birthday at the end of June.

They describe Montpellier in such extravagantly enthusiastic terms that we begin to imagine its winding streets and walled Renaissance gardens, its sunlit fountains and avenues of plane trees. We see ourselves with French friends sitting at outdoor cafés and dining at fine restaurants, going to the opera, visiting art galleries, sunning ourselves on Mediterranean beaches and hiking through a landscape dotted with ruined châteaux. We believe the French family's claim that schools are excellent and that hospitals, should we fall ill, are beyond compare, as Montpellier is home to the oldest and best medical school on the continent. In Montpellier we will find culture, learning, pleasure—yes, happiness. We convince ourselves, after their recital of virtues, that this "total French immersion" will equip us to return to Ottawa—and the job market—as proper, fully bilingual Canadians.

In Montpellier that autumn, not far from where we rent a small house near the university, I discover an ice rink open all year round. I skate there on Tuesday afternoons when it is nearly empty, and I take the old Walkman along, for it pleases me to be skating again to the *Graceland* cassette, even though there's usually amplified pop music echoing around the arena, playing havoc with my ears.

Still, I persist. For it makes me think of Africa in another way now than I did when I was skating around the outdoor oval of ice in Ottawa. It makes me remember sullen little Grace, for whom I always had to play *Graceland* in the car, because once I had been in a silly mood and had shown her the plastic container and had said, "Look, Grace. This is your own country. Grace-Land." And after that, she would get in the car in the morning and want it put in the tape deck, repeating the word until I did so. She would never talk to me, or to my daughter, but she seemed a little less woebegone while the music was playing. How odd, I'd muse, that the ludicrous mansion of Elvis has been transported to this place where it exists as something rare and beautiful in the mind of Grace. As if this transformation made for some kind of redemption.

Soon after we are settled in France, I receive a letter from Rachel, telling me about her latest trials with Lois, how well Ronnie is doing in school and how badly poor Grace. She wonders if I can send her anything to help out but adds she will understand if I can't find a way. I write back and say of course I will try, but I don't do it immediately. A few weeks later, there is another letter. This one is shorter and more direct. It says that she has "something bad in her blood" and must spend time in Kenyatta Hospital on this account. She is desperate for money.

I figure out a system to get cash to her—Ruth, who would have been the obvious choice, is now in South Africa, where her journalist husband is covering the ongoing saga of apartheid's demise—and then I don't hear from her at all. I wonder why she's felt she had to make up such a story about her blood in order to get money. Didn't she know I'd give it? Rachel is so large and healthy-looking that I can't imagine anything wrong with her.

But I am mistaken. She has leukemia, and there is no chance for recovery. I learn this not from Rachel but from Ruth, who has heard from a volunteer at Nairobi Hospice, who says that Rachel's on her care list and is rapidly dying. I send letters to Rachel, but I never hear from her again, and it is Bridgid who writes to tell me that Rachel has died. I think of Bridgid's warmth and kindness, and hope it was she who cared for Rachel at the end. I think of sad little Grace, so hopeless and glum, and Ronnie with his plucky spirit and winning ways. And tough, vulnerable Lois, and the old parents sitting bent on their bench and stool outside the house, who must be waiting now to join their dead daughter. I can think of no way to help them from so far away. I know no one in Nairobi now who might walk down that track: the political and social climate has worsened in the year since we left, and violent theft—carjackings, burglaries, muggings—is on the rise. Carrying cash out to a village? Impossible.

"Don't worry so," Bob says, seeking to comfort me. "The family will be cared for by their own people. They are not your responsibility. Remember, Rachel's church will have a *harambee,* it will be okay." He is not heartless—he is committed, after all, to helping people in developing countries—but he is a realist and he knows there are limits. Even Ruth, a woman with a heart so large that eventually she is given the Order of the British Empire for her hospice work, writes the same thing in a letter. "We can only do so much," she says. "We must just do what we can."

There is nothing for me to do now but to remember Rachel—I can see that. She is dead, and nothing I might have done could have prevented her from dying. Still, her death seems enormously hard to accept. Rachel is dead, I keep repeating to myself, and what that means, I slowly begin to understand, is that I am mourning Kenya as much as I am grieving for her. As I am saying this, I am at the ice rink with *Graceland* in the Walkman and such sadness in my heart that I feel I could die. But of course I don't. I just keep skating round and round and round.

GOING TO BANAUE

MY METHOD FOR GETTING through life has generally been as follows: if I want to block people from something they want, not only must I have good reason for my negative stance, I must offer some alternative plan equal in weight and value. Since the early years of our marriage, it has been established that my career, writing and teaching writing, is tied to whatever talent I have and not to progress in some organization or university. Because of this I've been willing to accompany Bob from place to place, and it has worked surprisingly well.

But the cat and I hate it here in the Philippines. We convey this heresy to each other by the merest flick of our eyelids, me stretched out on the couch and Ballou lying on the floor at my feet. The thick, humid air makes it too hot to move, too heavy and sticky for him to lie on my lap and be petted as I read—and we're thrown off a comfortable routine we've known for nearly a decade. He sprawls on his back and twitches his tail as he watches a skinny gecko hotfoot it across the ceiling, but he knows better than to get all excited. He'd never get the gecko. It's too damn hot to even think about it, anyway.

When we decided to come here in 1993, the contract in Montpellier had ended. A job offer for Bob from the International Rice Research Institute was irresistible, for it would take him right to retirement age. We knew the move to the Philippines would provide us with a chance to learn more about Asia, and we were sure that the experience would be exciting and enriching, just as France and Kenya had been. We expected that, because we had made major cultural adjustments twice before, this time would be easier. But we discover, to our chagrin, that we are wrong and it is much harder.

The truth is, this weather doesn't suit us. Not the cat, nor me, nor the rest of the family. We were made for a more northerly clime than Los Baños, south of Manila on the island of Luzon. We tell ourselves we never suffered like this in Kenya, for Nairobi lies on a high plateau above sea level and, even when days are hot, nights are cool and refreshing. Although Mombasa and Lamu on the coast were steamy, we remember gentle breezes off the Indian Ocean, ruffling the palm trees and soothing the spirit. We admit we experienced blazing Mediterranean heat in Montpellier, but there, we recall, the dry air sparkled and was never damp and oppressive. It was never like *this*. After several months in the Philippines, we are glum and defeated.

Of course we can see that this landscape is lushly beautiful, in a breathless, tropical sort of way. None of us is immune to the beauty of orchids and butterflies, or to sunlight in the garden sliding off banana leaves like melted butter. Nevertheless, my homesick heart is stubborn, and night after night I dream of snow.

Bob and I decide to go up into the mountains of northern Luzon while Abbey is visiting school friends in France during the Christmas holidays: she's miserable, and we hope this trip will restore her good humour. We know we won't find snow, but it will be cooler in the Cordillera, and we'll be able to walk for pleasure. Every time we try to climb Mount Makiling, the extinct volcano wrapped in luxuriant rain forest overlooking Los Baños, we turn back after an hour, our faces and bodies streaming with sweat and our tempers frazzled.

We're also going north to see the ancient Ifugao rice terraces of Banaue, which we have learned to pronounce Bah-nah-way. Even before arriving in the Philippines we'd heard about this "eighth wonder of the world" and although I am prepared to be disappointed—in my experience, scenic spots seldom live up to advance notices—I am relieved to be leaving the staff compound of the rice institute, home to sixty other families like ourselves who have come from abroad. Inside its gates are pleasant lawns and gardens surrounding large, airy houses, but I cannot accustom myself to the enclosed space: all I can see are the high walls on which shards of glass glitter in the sun.

We set off well before five in the morning in order to get through Manila before traffic jams the route, as it does each day by six. As dawn breaks through dark cloud, the highway is already densely packed with diesel-belching trucks and cars, and on the dirt shoulders thousands of people are walking to work or running to catch overloaded buses and jeepneys. In the smoky half-light, it is a scene from hell.

The distance to Banaue is three hundred and fifty kilometres but it will take us ten hours to get there, slowed not only by urban congestion but by the road itself, its surface eroded and pitted by torrential rains and transport trucks. As we go farther north, we encounter damage from the killer earthquake of 1991—at one point, the old road simply disappears and the rough detour through a dry riverbed is now permanent. Farther still into hill country, we skirt fallen boulders big as houses, and edge around great slides of dark red mud, much of it alarmingly fresh.

Through the silvery drizzle that accompanies us all day, it has been possible to see the geographic features of Luzon altering dramatically. Excitement stirs my blood: I can feel the mountains coming. By the time the bright green rice paddies are hours behind us, coconut palms have also disappeared and the earth is opening up to the sky. Like a child's primer in perspective, brown fields of rice stubble stretch off to meet blown-out old volcanoes, dark as aubergines in the distance. We pass over wide riverbeds recently flooded during typhoon season but already drying up—in places, the water is only a trickle through pale gravel. The only bits of colour in this grim stonescape are village women crouching beside silty water, washing clothes, laying them out flat to dry on the rocks even in the rain—where else to put them? Sooner or later the sun will come out. It is this cheery accommodation to climate I tell myself I must make too. Sooner or later.

By the time we get through narrow mountain passes to Banaue, night is nearly upon us. The valley is stuffed with fog and it is impossible to see the terracing. We can only make out the immediate town itself: a jostle of corrugated metal shacks set on concrete stilts on the hillside, and a few other more substantial cement-block buildings—a church, a clinic, a school—forming a core at the bottom of the hill. In the rain, the overall effect is dismal and desolate.

We elect to stay in a *pension* called the Spring Village Inn, and indeed the spring splashes noisily down right outside our bedroom window. The wood-panelled room smells like linseed oil. The single ceiling bulb sheds just enough light for Bob to begin reading his Christmas present, *Johnson and Boswell in Scotland,* a choice more appropriate to these highlands than my new Gordimer. We have brought extra pillows, fruit-cake, and a bottle of celebratory malt whisky for New Year's Eve and our wedding anniversary. We consider holing up in the room until our books are read and our supplies have run out but, after an hour, curiosity and hunger propel us into the dark, muddy streets where rain falls in glistening sheets. We get soaked right through before we find a small food bar halfway down the hill, little more than a cement hall with a handful of tables. The rice with curried vegetables is hot and delicious and we eat with gusto.

Over tea, we look around at the other customers, local families. We are amused because we are wearing hiking boots while they are wearing flip-flops on their bare feet. Ifugao people are shorter and darker than their compatriots to the south, and their faces bring to mind their counterparts in the mountains of Nepal or Guatemala, solemn to the point of being stern. I feel as if I am in a different country, not just a different part of Luzon.

Walking down the street later, we poke into tiny shops selling woodcarvings, baskets and weaving, handicrafts for which Banaue is famous. We stop at one visibly different from the others—merchandise is arranged artfully on the shelves, and the objects have been chosen from all over the archipelago. We strike up a conversation with a sweet-faced man pumping a sewing machine at the back of the shop. He explains that the shop is run by a foundation that funds an orphanage run by one person, a Frenchman named Antoine. We ask if we might meet him and visit the children.

The next morning is as inclement as the night before, and we don rainproof gear before going out. However, in the daylight it is possible to peer through the mist and see the slopes around and above the village. We are suitably impressed, awed by the vastness of what we see: for a change, reality is not disappointing. These Banaue terraces are only a small portion of those in the surrounding mountains which, the guidebook assures us, if laid end to end would measure fourteen thousand kilometres, or nearly half the circumference of the earth. There is some academic argument about the age of the terracing, two schools of thought at opposite ends of a spectrum that runs from two thousand years ago to a mere four hundred, the latter position supported, oddly enough, by *lack* of evidence: there was no mention made of terraces by early Spanish invaders who came here in search of gold. Nonetheless, there is something ancient and timeless in the way the wild and rocky mountainsides have been tamed into a giant garden. Each individual terrace fits itself to the incline and the contour—as well as to those above and below—and the resulting whole is harmonious, graceful, satisfying.

Unlike the grand monuments of Europe, these terraces are not about conventional power—religious or royal or political—but they do testify to the dominance of rice in Asia. The scene is ripe with irony, for although it appears that man has taken over the wilderness and is controlling nature, it is clear that the real power lies not with the Ifugao people but with the grain they put in their stomachs. Their entire existence is regulated by it, tied to it, springs from it: from the growing of rice they derive their gods, their calendar, their social system, their livelihoods.

These terraces are so tranquil it's hard to believe that until the early part of this century the Ifugao were headhunters, settling most disputes by taking the losers' heads home. Like hillbillies everywhere, they seem to have been a cranky lot, fiercely territorial and protective of their terraces that were, in every sense, their wealth. I am unsettled, thinking about this bloody business. How is it, I wonder, that bland rice can excite men to hack off their enemies' heads? But then, if these first months in the Philippines have taught me anything, it is that this is a country of such juxtaposition and contrast the only thing you ever know for certain is that logic is not the tool with which to dig out meaning. This morning, for example, I pick up the *Philippine Daily Inquirer* to find the usual mélange of rape-slay and tax-scam stories playing second fiddle to a headline report of another typhoon. At the bottom of the page, however, I find a happier story, about the increase in Marian visitations.

There has been an avalanche of miracles recently in the Philippines, as the Mother of God has been appearing all over the country, curing the faithful and warning the godless, doing her Marian thing. In one place, she drove the sun into a frenzied dance across the sky; in another, she transformed the Communion host in a young boy's mouth into flesh and blood. Bleeding statues, hovering visions, weeping trees— miracles here are as common as grass; fodder for the media, food for the masses. There's a hunger, a lust for the miraculous—people turn out in the hundreds of thousands to wait for apparitions in a farmer's field, they fill stadiums to witness faith healers. There's something about life here that gives rise to a unique hybrid of animism, superstition and Catholicism, resulting in the certainty that anything, *anything* can happen.

Sometimes anything turns out to be earthquakes and volcanoes and typhoons working together in a kind of fiendish partnership—the floods following a storm can set in motion mudslides in mountain areas shaken by recent tremors, or, in another ghastly variation, rain washes volcanic ash down the sides of Mount Pinatubo, turning it to *lahar*, a deadly grey mud flowing across sugarcane fields and burying whole villages. In a country where calamity knows every trick in the book and nature loves to play dirty, maybe miracles provide a necessary, heavenly balance. Anything can happen. It is that simple and that complicated.

The tailor guides us to the orphanage on the edge of Banaue, where Antoine owns some land on which he has built metal-roofed houses in native style—dormitories and a kitchen—and his own house, a fine old Ifugao thatched *bale*, standing on high wooden stilts. Dismantled and moved from a mountain village and then rebuilt here, it is home for Antoine and two small Filipino children he has adopted: Melchior, two, and Sarah, four.

He is a tall, thin man with a ragged moustache, wearing a shabby brown pullover. When we meet him, he's boiling water over an open fire and immediately offers us tea. We are urged to sit down and soon have both children and their kittens in our laps. We begin politely in French but soon move to English when it becomes clear that he is bilingual and that conversation can progress more easily this way.

I am openly inquisitive, asking a string of questions that he answers with the calm of a man resigned to doling out details of his life to strangers. Born in Basel but raised in Biarritz, he began travelling the world when he was twenty and has lived outside France for seventeen years. Sometimes he stops in one place, as he did in Calcutta, where he spent two years working with Mother Theresa. He has been in the Philippines for several years and after visiting Banaue decided he wanted to stay, taking all his money to create a refuge for needy children. As he goes through his tale, he smokes cigarettes in need of constant relighting—it is a wet day, the dampness all pervasive. I wish I had a fresh dry pack of Gitanes for him.

In his first Banaue summer, he brought more than two hundred children from the slums of Manila so that they could spend time in the cool and unpolluted air of the mountains. Predictably, most were restless, anxious to get back to their familiar haunts—but the idea had taken hold in Antoine's mind. He made arrangements to provide a permanent home for twenty-three children, either orphaned or from desperately poor families.

"But how did you accomplish this?" I ask, imagining all kinds of logistic and legal problems.

"I just made myself available," he says. And then, with a smile indicating it is a phrase he often uses, adds, "If your desire is deeply rooted in your heart, everything is possible."

Antoine explains that he raised funds by writing to one hundred friends asking for money. Miraculously, most of his letters were answered and, even more miraculously, people continue to send assistance regularly. Money comes as he needs it, he says. At the very beginning, a young French-Canadian woman volunteered to help for a year, and she has been followed by Europeans; it is necessary, he says, to have a "feminine sensibility present" when raising teenage girls.

His luminous, deep-set eyes are the dominant feature of his thin face, commanding attention even as he speaks in a soft voice. He is so ascetic in appearance that he seems more like a priest or a monk than the father of two rollicking Filipino infants. He tells how his efforts to improve the health of his children by renovating the clinic in Banaue have led to the establishment of a small preschool and childcare centre. He is busy every minute now, he says, because there is always more to do. Besides running the craft shop, he has organized various projects for the older children so that they can be financially independent when they come of age. He has set up a tricycle-taxi business for the boys, and a furniture-making studio, and has just begun a new project for making garden pots in the shape of the stern and brooding rice god Bul-ul. Carved out of fern roots, the black figures are about half a metre high with indentations in their crowns into which flowerpots can be set. Because they are so distinctive and light to carry, tourists are rapidly buying and carting them off. All this preparation is

for his eventual departure, Antoine says.
will return to Europe and, with that in
already studying law by correspondence.
His presence in Banaue is a kind of miracle, I say, and
he laughs at such a notion. "Really, what do the people
here think of you?" I ask, and he says I must ask *them*,
for it is not for him to say. I do so later, and the answer
is the same from each person: "He is a missionary,"
they say, and they do not mean that he is converting the
children but that he is a saintly man.

Next day the clouds hang low, as if they might burst
any moment. Nevertheless, we hire a jeepney to take
us out into the neighbouring valleys where the terraces
are even more spectacular and where life in the remote
villages has remained essentially unchanged over centuries. The road is horribly rough—my head bangs
against the metal roof as we bounce over rocks and
into potholes—but worse than the bone-rattling
bumps is the road's narrowness: there are moments
when it seems there's not much more than a grass
blade between our wheels and a drop of several hundred metres. I try to keep my focus on the distant landscape, paying attention to how the terraces curve
around the mountainsides in such a sinuous fashion;
the design is both elaborate and simple, fluid lines

curling and swirling out and then back again, artistic flourishes to perfect agricultural order imposed on hostile terrain.

The jeepney has taken us to a rise overlooking the valley of Banga-an where we will walk for the afternoon. The driver suggests that we visit the small hotel where he will wait for us, and on his advice we order pots of tea and bowls of rice from Conchita, the elfin proprietor, who has erected a traditional granary on stilts, called an *alang*, near the hotel. She invites us to climb up inside, where she shows us bright gold bundles of rice grain stored up in the dark rafters, and gives us a taste of *bayah*, sweet rice wine she makes by mixing roasted grain and yeast and letting the fermented mash drip through a filter of leaves into a pot.

When we start down into Banga-an, the sensation is of entering a green bowl of music. The walls of the valley circumvolve like a repetitive melody, the visual equivalent of Ravel's "Bolero" or Pachebel's "Canon." However, being in and on the terraces is very different from viewing them from afar, for the trail is steep and slippery and the footing precarious along the tops of the wet stone walls. I felt gigantic sitting next to tiny Conchita on the floor of the *alang*, and here again I feel huge and clumsy—these walkways have been made for small Ifugao feet, not mine.

As we clamber down the hillside we spot the bent figure of someone planting seedlings in a rice paddy

near the village of Banga-an at the bottom. We guess it
is a woman, and as we descend we see we were right—
hardly surprising, since we know that, in most villages,
men and boys leave to make money elsewhere, and
only women, children and the elderly remain at home.
This woman, who appears to be old, is wearing a red
cardigan over a dark blue dress and has a bamboo
coolie hat tied on her head with a red plastic ribbon. It
seems a fancy fashion accent, that ribbon. She never
straightens as she works to her own steady rhythm,
taking seedlings from a bright green bunch held in one
hand and sticking them firmly down into the watery
mud with the other.

When we reach the village in the centre of the valley,
we are tired, and sit on a log. The old woman looks
over and throws us a vermilion, betel-nut-stained
smile. Her thin face is wrinkled with sun and age, and
she looks far too frail to be working as hard as she is.
We realize, as we climb back to the top of the terraces,
that perhaps three hours have passed and that she has
not stopped planting in all that time.

Banaue fades like Brigadoon once we are home in Los
Baños, and within a day or two it is difficult to
remember the thrill of being cold and wet, walking in
the mountains. Again I complain to Ballou about the

heat, and again I dream of snow. But also in my dream now is the bent figure of the old lady planting seedlings in the paddy, working without pause except, now and again, to adjust the red ribbon of her hat. It becomes clear to me, in the way that things become perfectly obvious in dreams, that she alone is responsible for the terraces, that she has built them and now farms them entirely on her own. Like the little red hen she has done it—miraculously—all by herself.

Awake, I think not of the terraces but of Antoine and his orphans. We elect to be among the number of his friends who send money, and at intervals we also send chocolate and cigarettes with people going to Banaue on business from the rice institute. Once, they come back bearing a gift from Antoine: two Bul-ul pots, which we fill with flowers and set by the front door. But in the four years remaining for us in the Philippines, although we correspond by mail and talk to him by telephone, we never return to the mountains and we never see him again.

Along with a variety of other souvenirs from the Philippines, the Bul-ul pots will eventually make their way to France, where they now guard the stone steps to our house, Mas Blanc. Every spring I plant rosy red verveine in their heads and think about Antoine, and the orphanage in Banaue. Mostly, however, I continue to wonder how it is that compassionate goodness wells up in one person and not in another.

Over time, my remembrance of the tall Frenchman mingles with the image of the little old lady on the terraced hillside of Banga-an, two figures juxtaposed in a strange and lovely collage. She, working simply to eat, is creating a landscape of astounding beauty. He, believing that one person can make a difference, is changing the world. Together, they teach me that anything can happen and everything is possible.

SOMEDAY YOU'LL BE SORRY

EVEN AS I AM GETTING OUT my credit card to pay for the duty-free eau de toilette on the Air France flight from Paris to Toronto, I am aware what a telling choice it is, the small pale blue bottle on which is written *Remember ME*. Isn't this what we all want—to be read? Isn't this what writers want, to be read and reread, to remain in print? Besides, the older I get, the more I seem to need the past to give heft and weight to the present. Gone is the youthful longing for *fast forward*: I keep hitting *rewind*.

The bottle of scent, however, is an insipid shade, too passive a hue to represent my passionate engagement with nostalgia. I gather that this particular colour is meant to bring to mind forget-me-nots, those delicate flowers growing wild in the fields and tame in the gardens of Europe and North America. They were my favourite flower when I was a child, perhaps because I was allowed to pick as many as I liked where they bloomed in blue profusion under the pear trees behind Auntie Dot's house on Hampton Street. She wasn't really my aunt, she was my mother's best friend and she'd come up out of the great United States to live in our little town of Elmira where her husband, Charlie, worked with my father, Ron, at the Naugatuck chemical plant.

Simply by writing their names—Charlie and Dot— I am swept by a wave of emotion back into one clear moment sitting at the kitchen table in that house on Hampton Street, making a bouquet of forget-me-nots. A red-brick house that always smelled of coffee and buttered toast, it is a place I cannot get back to in memory without going through the painful sensation— emotional anguish so real it seems physical—of exile and loss. Well, we are all exiled from childhood, that's no news. How is it that some people march forward but others of us look back and ache with longing?

The moment at the table dissolves into another. The summer I was nearly five and my sister, Ruthie, was born, I was left for long periods with Auntie Dot, who helped prepare me for September kindergarten by using her dishes to teach numbers and colours. Each piece of brightly glazed earthenware was one solid colour, either a rich, dense primary or vivid orange or green. Still, all these years later, I can touch in memory the fluted rim of a cobalt blue plate and hear Dot's distinctive chuckly voice telling me "blue" and feel her warm freckled hand on mine, showing me how to form the letter *B* with a crayon. The edges of this recollection waver out and blur into nothingness, but that notion of "blue," which encompasses so much more than colour, is wedged like a plate in my brain.

Occasionally I am asked what it's like to have such precise memories of childhood, the question assuming that fiction I have written about growing up in the 1950s is autobiographical and the result of total recall. But in truth, my ability to remember is not dependable; it is sporadic and fragmented. Images seldom sustain themselves longer than a few seconds—brief flashes of sensation, confused and confusing. Generally, it is my own emotional state that comes back with more clarity than details surrounding occasion or place or people.

To authenticate the memories above, I send an email query to Dot's daughter Valerie, now in her sixties and living in Connecticut, besides phoning my sister in England to check a few facts with her. I could "get" the way the house smelled but not the name of the street. "Yes, there were pear trees," Valerie writes, but she is uncertain whether the forget-me-nots grew beneath them or beside the house. I decide, with the well-meaning arrogance of a fiction writer, to leave them where I wish them to be.

Memory: 1953, I am ten and in a sulk in the backseat of the family Plymouth as we drive out of Elmira and up Highway 86, a narrow two-lane road heading northwest toward Lake Huron. I hate this regular Sunday trip to see my father's mother in Chesley, or my mother's brothers and sisters—my uncles and aunts and cousins—in Listowel, Wingham and Ripley. These little country towns, none of them larger than Elmira with its population of two thousand, are each half an hour apart "up the line." My mother's family calls Highway 86 "the line" and I imagine it as a long cord, knotted every so often with an uncle or an aunt. We are tied to the line and that's what irks me. I don't see the point of spending so much time with people simply because they're related. It's not that I dislike my relatives—I am very fond of my cousins—but my mother's clannishness gets me down. I never mind Christmas visits, fat-fingered Uncle Frank playing fiddle while we children swirl crazily up and down Aunt Norma's living room in imitation of a Scottish reel, but these talky Sundays of pot roast and pudding? Boring.

I find the landscape passing by the car window equally pointless and without charm. Cornfields, pasture, swamps, maple bush, barns and silos, big brick houses with wide front porches at the end of long lanes—it's all the same. Boring. I feel suffocated by this rich green farmland, cooped up and fenced in. Oh, I can't wait until I am old enough to leave home and then I'll be off. Oceans are what I want, and snow-covered mountains, huge cities and jungles and deserts, people of different colour wearing clothes of every stripe, speaking strange languages that fall on the ear like rain. Is that too much to ask?

In my most petulant tone I confide this desire, or something like it, to my parents in the front seat. Little Ruthie, age five, listens with some alarm to the heated discussion that ensues, during which I state my position more firmly and my mother chides me for lack of gratitude and family feeling. "Someday you'll be sorry, young lady," she says. And in her most ominous tone, she adds, "You'll find out there's nothing more important than family and the place where you grew up. You just wait and see."

Did she really say that, or have I invented these lines? Oh, I am sure she did, not only once but many times, as I exhibited over the years such restless discontent with where—and who—I was. Neither my mother nor Judy Garland in *The Wizard of Oz* could make me believe that "there's no place like home" was a positive statement about life. I was bitterly disappointed by Dorothy and Toto's return to Kansas: it seemed an awful letdown, a nasty cheat. But then, I knew that's the way things were.

I'd been to Toronto a few times, to stay with a child-less aunt and uncle who enjoyed cosseting their numerous nieces and nephews and who seemed happy to satisfy our every whim. I was an easy guest on these occasions, for I was content simply to be there—Toronto was the Emerald City, alive with splendour and surprise. But just when I'd be feeling that I might stay forever, it'd be time to go home and I'd be filled with sadness. In Elmira there were no clanging street-cars, no museum full of mummies, no Murray's for tin-roof sundaes, no strolling on the boardwalk by the lake to look at the glittering city lights at night.

During the 1950s—simpler times, simpler pleas-ures—my parents frequently had friends over for musical evenings: my father on piano (unless Myrtle was present, in which case he played slide whistle and she took keyboard), Hugh and Morley on fiddle, Dot and Charlie singing alto and tenor harmonies, my mother taking up her customary position on the sofa as appreciative audience. (Early in their courtship my musical father had expressed his opinion that she could not carry a tune, and so she did not sing except in church in a low and self-conscious way. Even in the car on Sunday trips when we'd sing rounds she seldom joined in, convinced that she would put us off. It could break your heart, remembering this.)

My sister and I would park ourselves quietly behind the closed hall door and listen to the songs and late-night laughter, but I was often troubled by how many songs had to do with *home*. Had my mother arranged the program for my benefit? She was that determined, she might have. From "Home on the Range" to "My Old Kentucky Home" to her favourite, "I'll Take You Home Again, Kathleen," these songs, to my mind, were nothing but sentimental slosh and all part of a losing campaign to convince me to be like her and to stay in Elmira forever. I preferred the lyrics to "The Whiffenpoof Song" or "On the Road to Mandalay," and would wait sleepily behind the door until they got round to these, as they always did toward the end of the evening. Doomed from here to eternity, I'd slide blissfully off to bed, with the dawn coming up like thunder in my dreams. . . .

I've lived abroad now for more than fifteen years, and I've seen oceans and deserts and people with skin both lighter and darker than mine. But every summer I have made a point of *going home* to the various places in Ontario where I've lived—and with each trip I find myself spiralling down deeper into the past, searching for some thing or some place I fear may be invisible. It is becoming a bit of an obsession, this quest to know what and where home is.

Each year I fly back to teach fiction writing in
Toronto at the end of July, and then take August to
drive around the province within a rectangle formed by
London, Haliburton, Ottawa and Belleville, seeing
friends and cousins and two remaining aunts by marriage. There is no immediate family to visit, for my
mother died in 1974 and my father in 1991. Nor is my
sister in Canada, for she married an Englishman the
same year that I married my bearded Scot, and lives in
Yorkshire: it still baffles us that we both fell in love with
men named Bob with whom we have settled elsewhere.
As if we are getting our comeuppance for having abandoned our native land, there is no "family home" to
which we can return: the house where we grew up—a
white stucco bungalow across from the high school—
belongs to my father's second wife, from whom we are
estranged.

But it is home I want, home I lust for, home I want
to remember in perfect detail. I cannot hear "I'll Take
You Home Again, Kathleen" without being seized by
wistful longing. I have learned to play it on the piano
and I often do so, late at night.

Actually, it is not that small white house I mean
when I write the word *home*, but the subtle kinetic
familiarity that comes from situating oneself in recognizable terrain, the feeling of *knowing who you are*.
Ironically, it is the hated Sunday route to see the relatives, slicing through Mennonite farmland northwest

of Toronto, that gives me the strongest sense of physical location and returns me to my youthful self. Every few years, and again this summer—half a century after those fierce arguments—here I am alone in a rented car, driving up Highway 86, passing through town after town, going up the line. Although I am at the wheel, in my heart I am in the back seat again, with Ruthie snuggled up against me, sleeping.

I take note that although the highway is much improved, still two lanes but widened, the landscape here has not changed, and I am grateful to see nothing but corn and more corn on both sides of the road—it's all just the same as I remember. But these undulating dark green fields bring to mind my vegetarian daughter in lecture mode, voicing her disapproval of land being used to feed cattle and pigs. Suddenly, I remember myself as a kid, climbing over a rail fence and ripping a cob from its stalk, wanting to know what "cow corn" tasted like. Tearing the green leaves away, I took a bite and felt my mouth fill with chalky, starchy juice as I chewed the tough kernels. It was a nasty, flat taste, but I had the idea that, if I had to, I could survive by eating it. My imagination, always fertile, now added cow corn to acorns and clover blossoms on my list of possible foods—if war came, if I were poor, if I were on the run, making my final escape.

How I longed for anonymity. To be on a train going somewhere in the night (the sound of the whistle, the sound of the wheels), the pure romance of solitude within a crowd—that's what I wanted. This wish to be unknown, what was that but a reaction to growing up in a town where everyone knew your business? Where, if you strayed, there'd be someone to find you and bring you home.

For my twenty-first birthday—September 21, 1964—I asked for, and received, the present I wanted: airfare to New York. The hundred-dollar bill my father gave me also paid for part of my accommodation in the old Taft Hotel and I used money from my summer job for the rest. I flew down at the end of August, just before I'd be going back to university for my final year, and had four full days to explore the city. The weather was hot and heavy, but my spirits were light as I walked up and down the Avenues, across and back again on the Streets, learning the map of Manhattan by heart and by foot. My mother, worried about my being alone, had sewn a small pocket in my brassiere in which to keep a dime for the emergency phone call she was sure would come. My father, who occasionally went to New York on business, gave me three typewritten sheets of information, including the location of several washrooms so that I wouldn't ever have to speak to strangers in order to find one. They told me not to forget to call home.

Of course I forgot. I forgot them, and home, and who I was and where I was from, and thus was free to invent another self entirely fabricated from desire. This other self—strikingly beautiful, first play opening on Broadway any day soon—blossomed in my head as I walked. I was not deluded, but I dwelled within the daydream and saw everything through it, as if I'd been transformed magically from innocent bumpkin to confident urban person who belonged in New York.

In this slightly euphoric mood I decided to dine at the one restaurant I knew, having been to the city once before with my family: Howard Johnson's on Times Square. I was dressed in a smart little two-piece outfit with orange linen high-heeled shoes, remnants from my last stint as bridesmaid—many friends had married that summer—and I ordered a martini and a plate of fried clams. Spearing my olive in worldly fashion, I smiled at the motherly waitress as she brought the clams, imagining that she was looking at me as if wondering whether she'd seen my photo in *The New York Times*. And indeed, she smiled back, and bent toward me: "Now where are *you* from, dear?"

I sometimes tell this anecdote for laughs, mocking my youth and naïveté (Howard Johnson's, for heaven's sake), and to demonstrate how much I wanted to be someone else and to be that someone elsewhere. Yet everything about that story shows how I could not escape what I was—a decent daughter who wouldn't have dreamed of *really* running away to New York, and who was willing to settle for a good deal less than adventure. The embarrassment and shame of white, middle-class privilege I have so often felt in adulthood seems but a social refinement of that much earlier chagrin: I knew I was a very ordinary small-town girl with big dreams but little nerve. A *home girl* at heart. Funny, after all these years that's what I am, although I'm far from home.

I see that although I started out to write about *going home,* so far this is less about place than it is about memory and personal history. Even though that shift has been an unconscious veering off-course, it's no accident: the act of returning, as everyone knows who has gone away, is an attempt to know oneself, just as the initial departure sprang from the same source. You think it's the landscape you want to see again, but really you're looking for yourself. Coming back to the place you are from, after a long absence, you see things the way they were, not as they are—you come face to face with surprising ghosts, invisible to everyone else, and some of the ghosts wear your face.

I cruise through the old hometown and catch, out of the corner of my eye—just a flash as I drive by—myself at ten, getting off my bicycle outside the

Carnegie Library ready to deal with the librarian who forbids me to read books from the Adult Section. There I am again, standing on the corner of South Street, pulse racing and cheeks burning, discussing the meaning of happiness with the handsome history teacher who suggests *The Life of Socrates* as my Grade 11 essay topic and sets me on my way. Then at the foot of Erb Street, I bump into myself at six, running to escape a small mob of children pelting me with snowballs and calling me names. Everywhere I look, ghosts.

I see who I have become in these visions of who I've been, moments that would have been obliterated if I had stayed, rubbed smooth or obscured by quotidian layers of encounter. When you remain in a place, the blur of experience makes it difficult, impossible even, to sift through and retrace individual moments. The sands of time solidify so that there is only the *now* occurring at the top of accumulated (and thus invisible) history. You know the past is there, of course, but you can't get to it—you'd be driven mad if every trip down Arthur Street involved remembering every other one. Absence brings its own reward: these dreamlike flashes are my compensation, ephemeral enough to become fiction.

Because we were raised in an era when it was more common for families to stay in one place, the girls with whom I went to kindergarten were pretty much the same girls with whom I left high school, as we sailed off to university or teachers' college or nurses' training. Most of us married, most of us had children, many of us stayed within a stone's throw of Elmira, and although some of us strayed across the country or around the world, we have never been entirely lost or forgotten. Christmas cards, phone calls, occasional visits—the same girls who'd been best friends in high school maintained connections, with enough overlapping of twos and threes that each of us continues to be woven into a flimsy but enduring web of friendship.

The summer we all turned fifty, one of us planned a reunion to which she invited a dozen women: ten of us arrived at her home for a slumber party, just as we'd done on countless weekends in various attics and basement rec rooms during our teens. Without husbands or children or grandchildren, we basked in the easy warmth of childhood familiarity, telling the same old jokes we'd always told. We looked at high school yearbooks, reminisced about teachers, compared notes on boyfriends (some of us had married them), phoned absent friends, drank Diet Coke or white wine and listened to old LPs of Pat Boone and Jerry Lee Lewis. We were as noisy and raucous as teenagers all afternoon, but as night fell and we slipped into clusters of twos and threes, our voices became huskier and softer, the intimate murmur of women sharing their lives. Before bed, when everyone had gathered again in the living room, I was asked to read one of my short stories: the one I chose must have been too long, for the videotape made by the hostess shows most of those present asleep.

Next morning we were interviewed by a reporter from the local paper who wanted a human interest story about this bunch of aging dollies revisiting the past. I've saved the newspaper clipping with the photo of us in our nightgowns and pyjamas, squinting into the sunlight. We appear, to my eye, much younger than we are, our faces still plump and smooth, shining with happiness.

Since then, the reunions have been more frequent, and some women not at the initial party have appeared, just as others have not come back. Last summer eight of us met on a farm near Elmira: more photos of grandchildren, more news of illness, of widowhood and remarriage—but essentially, we agree, we're the same *girls*. One woman came from Saskatchewan: she and I had not met for more than forty years and might have passed each other on the street without recognition. Although we had been close as young girls, in high school she moved west and our correspondence dwindled: but she did not lose her connection to the group. During the afternoon, she and I sat together to catch up on our lives, and as we were talking I laughed the way I do, mouth wide open and head thrown back. She breathed a deep sigh of pleasure. "Goodness, you're like your mom," she said. "When you laugh like that I can see her."

My mother died when I was thirty and still defining myself as not-my-mother. Although I trace my looks and disposition to her side of our family rather than to my father's, I never thought I was like her: besides, she was a smaller woman, with finer features. Now, to be told there is a visible similarity, even if it's only our way of laughing? Wonderful. I *do* have something valuable of hers, after all, even if the things I thought I wanted—her crystal, her teacups, that hand-painted vase—are in the house I will never enter again.

Moved at my mother's being remembered after so long, I found my eyes filling with tears, and that made me laugh even more, for in this way I am indeed like her—she and her sisters used to weep buckets at the drop of a hat. Such a reaction was no surprise, given that my emotions were already highly charged—these gatherings of old friends seem hugely significant to me, as if we are living out the pages of a novel. I don't say this aloud, for one woman has already declared that I make too much of things. I've been accused of remembering events that no one else remembers and worse, of making things up—clearly, a fiction writer is not to be trusted. All of a sudden, I feel worried that some women here might believe I'd harm them by writing about these reunions.

It occurs to me that some of them might not even like me—but I don't care, I love them, every one. I love them for who they are and because we've known each other forever. They know me in a way I can never be known anywhere else. With them, I feel safe in that way you do when you are truly known, even when you also feel misjudged. I feel at home.

Later, driving through the farmland around Elmira, I have such a strong feeling of familiarity with the rural landscape that it seems I could close my eyes and still find the right direction, wherever I wanted to go. This chunk of southwestern Ontario, rimmed by three of the five Great Lakes, is overlaid by a tidy grid of county and township roads, thanks to those nineteenth-century surveyors with an orderly turn of mind. I know this region so well that I am sure I could draw a map from memory, placing Elmira exactly where it fits in proximity to cities such as Toronto and Guelph and Kitchener-Waterloo. If pressed, I could add several dozen surrounding towns and villages, so many of them named for homes left across the sea: Baden, Paris, Donegal, Brussels, Stratford—all Europe finds itself here, transformed. As I roll down the window and hang my elbow out, in my imagination there's a teenager at the wheel of the family automobile with "Wonderland by Night" blaring forth and scaring the cows along the backroads. But in reality there's a middle-aged woman thrilled that CBC radio is providing, at just the right moment, Beethoven's "Ode to Joy." She's singing at the top of her lungs, steering with one hand and conducting with the other out in the rushing air.

Coming into Elmira on 86, having made the turn north off Highway 7 near Guelph, I stop on the out-skirts of town, as I do most summers, to plant some-thing at the grave of my parents. My father, who died of lung disease in Florida, was cremated there after an autopsy, and has a flat name-stone that says RON over the place his urn is buried: my mother's upright stone, mottled rose-grey granite, states her name and age and station—wife of my father, whose second wife keeps the gravesite decorated with bouquets of plastic flow-ers. I am respectful enough that I do not move or destroy them, but always make my own gesture of remembrance, although my visits are too late in the season for planting and whatever I bring is dead by the next visit. But I like stopping on the way to buy ferns or ivy and a spoon for digging, and then turning off the highway into the maple-shaded domain of the cemetery to perform my small annual ritual.

Some years ago when I wrote my will I included a clause stating my wish to be cremated, as that seems an efficient method of allowing the body to assume its place in the greater scheme of things. I stipulated that money from my estate be used for someone to travel to the Hebrides where my mother's people are from, and to toss my ashes into the air and sea at the Butt of Lewis, top end of that rugged and wave-bashed Scottish island. I've always been one for the dramatic gesture. I'd do it myself if I could.

But as the years pass and I make these visits to my parents' graves, I feel my point of view changing and the will may have to be altered. If a year goes by without my managing to get to the cemetery, I feel oddly bereft and out of sorts, as if something important has not been done, as if something is missing. It surprises me beyond all measure that I attach deep feelings— memories, love, loss—to this place and to this polished slab of granite. I wouldn't want to deprive anyone remaining after me of the peculiar pleasure to be had in paying one's respects in this old-fashioned way.

After I finish the planting, and pull weeds and grass from around the stones, I walk around, recalling old schoolmates too early dead, or contemporaries of my parents, also gone. I read the names of these people out loud, as if to bring them back to mind with more force, and I conjure their faces as I stand by their stones. Merchants and doctors and teachers, young hockey players we thought would live forever, next-door neighbours familiar as tea after supper, several of my mother's women friends, and a number of foreigners who somehow landed in our town and died here, far from home.

The cemetery is situated on a rise of land overlooking the Canagagigue valley in which the chemical plant where my father worked still operates, no longer called Naugatuck but Uniroyal. The chemical waste buried around the plant in the 1940s and '50s eventually tainted not only the soil but also the water table, and by the 1980s various types of carcinogenic contamination had been traced in the aquifers around Elmira and in the waters of the Grand River into which the Canagagigue flows. Ironically, the dead have always been safe, up on the hill. Even more ironically, since the provincial inquiry forced a clean-up, an enormous shed in which dangerous wastes are stored has been erected across from the cemetery.

Refreshed by an hour of reflection, I get back in the car and, after a social call or two, drive out of Elmira and up 86 through Listowel, where my mother's elder brother used to sell insurance and real estate; his widow lives in Toronto. The town looks to be expanding and flourishing: although its downtown core is as it always was—two-storey brick buildings with glass storefronts—showy baskets of geraniums hang from the lampposts nowadays. I keep going, up through Wingham, where my mother's younger brother was a veterinarian. He died in middle age, and his remarried widow lives close by in the hamlet of Belgrave. I have promised to visit later in the week, but first I am going to Cousin Donald's cottage on Lake Huron, to the beach where, as a child, I gathered fossils with my father and where I learned to swim in the sandy shallows. Donald is the son of Aunt Norma, eldest of my mother's sisters, whose home in Ripley was the magnet drawing everyone up the line year after year, until she died in 1981.

A retired lawyer in his early seventies, Donald has spent summer at the lake since his childhood in Ripley, only ten minutes inland. His cottage, encircled with cedars, overlooks the beach in such a way that the view is limited to the horizon—sitting on the terrace and looking out, you are oblivious to other cottages along the beach. There is nothing to see but the wondrous way that water and sky change colour every few minutes, outdoing each other in shades of blue. I love this big, generous lake: as a child, I used to pretend it was the ocean and imagine myself setting off to sea.

One fine morning during my visit I persuade my cousin to join me for a swim, although he does not seem very eager and voices concern about the water temperature. "It's not cold once you're in," I fib, the way one does—and soon we are both splashing through the water out over the sandbars where we jump the white-capped waves together. When we finally stagger exhausted up to the cottage and rub ourselves dry with towels, we're laughing like children. The lake has washed away our years and our troubles, and made us young again.

After a couple of days I drive about forty kilometres northeast for my first visit to second cousins of my father. When I was growing up we never spent time with Dad's relatives except for my grandmother, whose ill health required our frequent visits to Chesley. Unlike my mother, my father did not come from a large family or have such a well-developed sense of tribal linkage; he seemed aloof from his past and uninterested in his ancestors, although on St. Patrick's Day he'd wear a green tie and claim some Irish heritage. However, ever since these elderly cousins came to his funeral service and met us, they have kept my sister and me involved in family correspondence, sending us genealogical material and faded sepia photographs of distant relatives we've never known.

They live in a grey faux-stone farmhouse set back from the road with spindly firs lining the lane. It is a scene so typical of this part of Ontario, I take several photos of the house and barn and the grazing cows in the adjacent field. Later, in the kitchen, I am served blackcurrant tea and biscuits, and told stories that illuminate something of my father's sad childhood, during which both his father and younger sister died of tuberculosis. They tell me how difficult it was for his mother when, after she was widowed, her dead husband's family turned its back and gave her no help at all. I sense that these nice people want me to understand something that remains unspoken, that they are explaining why my father appeared to lack "family feeling" and that I am meant to forgive him for that.

On the way to their farm I noted with pleasure how the landscape slowly changes from flat plains streaked with poplar windbreaks along the lake, where soybeans have largely replaced corn (I will remember to mention this to my daughter). Inland, the land begins to roll and swell into hills and valleys studded with bush and cedar. It is clear that the farms here are not so prosperous and that the soil is less rich. During the Wisconsin glacial period, melting ice must have pulled the good stuff down to Waterloo county where I come from: up here it's skimpy on the hilltops and swampy in the hollows.

I know all about that glacial stage because during my first year at university I took an introductory geology course, influenced by my early passion for collecting fossils. It turned out to be far more difficult than I'd expected, but I soldiered on to a final grade of D, rescued from complete failure by a splendid paper on the aforesaid glacier and its effect on my part of Ontario. To the essay I appended photos of drumlins and eskers between Elmira and Guelph, aided by my science-minded father who was pleased to assist me in this worthy venture—finding something in common made us both happy and relieved, as by that stage I had veered off into the dreamy realms of philosophy. We spent an entire Saturday driving around, looking for land formations we could label as drumlins (great mounds of gravel) or eskers (long barrow-like ridges).

I still hold in mind a stunningly clear image of my father standing on the roof of the car, snapping a photo of a drumlin that looked like a pretty little hill. Yet I doubt the memory, for it would have been very unlike him to do that. He was a quiet and cautious man, not given to extravagant gesture or dangerous showing off. Nevertheless, it is how I like to remember him, up there, snapping away, helping me pass my course. I think of that day when I turn onto 86 outside Guelph, even though the highway—straightened and widened —no longer goes through the same countryside. Or perhaps it does, but the terrain is unrecognizable because the drumlins have been reamed out, the gravel removed and the earth flattened, and the old fields of wheat and barley turned into real estate lots.

I am travelling with a camera so that I can take photos of my parents' birthplaces, both houses brick but as unlike in appearance and style as my parents were from each other. Before I leave, I ask Cousin Donald to drive with me a few kilometres inland from his cottage to look at the two-storey yellow-brick farmhouse where my mother was born, on the sixth concession outside Ripley, not far from Kincardine where she went to high school and got the Latin prize. She was the sixth of seven children born to a couple whose forbears had come during the last of the Scottish clearances and who settled with others from the same boat in this section of Bruce county. When my mother spoke of growing up on the sixth we were meant to understand "unique place" not just the number six— in much the way that the *sixième* in Paris means something definable to *Parisiens* who know the particular flavour of each *arrondissement*. For my mother and her kin, the sixth was nothing less than the centre of the universe.

I study the house, with its glassed-in front porch and its gladiola garden, from out on the road but am too shy to venture up the lane to ask if I might look around—besides, all I need to do is to peer from a distance to hear my mother's voice telling me about getting up to milk the cows before school, or about the team of horses that pulled the sleigh in winter—those stories I wouldn't listen to when I was young. Now I am trying to remember the names of those horses. She told us . . . but I didn't pay attention, and now the names are gone. Nor can my cousin remember.

I pester him with questions about other Scottish families who lived along the line and about what he recalls of our grandparents who died before I was born and what stories they might have told about *their* parents. But he does not recall stories. Not only did the immigrant generation bring few material possessions with them, they also seemed to care little for maintaining old ways. None of us cousins know any Gaelic today, it had disappeared from the family by our parents' time. *Close the Door* should have been our clan motto rather than *Dum Spiro, Spero*, the plucky Latin one ascribed to the MacLennans: While I breathe, I hope.

I visit the graveyard outside Ripley and take photos of the graves of grandparents and numerous other relatives and family connections. Many of them were dead long before my birth, but others come to mind vividly as I stand looking out past the rows of stones to the flat and featureless fields of grain beyond. Uncles and aunts and cousins from up and down the line, gone now, gone with all their stories never to be told or heard. The sadness I feel is deep and sharp, and I wish I could sing a lament in the language from where we came. Yes, Mother, you were right. I am sorry now.

Another day I drive into Chesley, my father's birthplace, which is, according to the sign at the town limits, "the nicest little town around." The squat red-brick house, not far from the cemetery where my paternal grandparents are buried, has undergone several changes over the years but its firm, cranky character is still intact, just as if red-haired Grandma was still inside. One large maple has been left shading the front of the house, but the wooden porch itself is new. In my grandmother's day the back garden had several rows of peony bushes that enabled her to donate bouquets to Chesley's churches from the end of May into July: now, however, the yard has been grassed over and there's some kind of repair garage beside the house.

This house, where Ruthie and I spent so many Sundays with our parents, haunts us. We sometimes play our very own "memory game" on the telephone, or when I am walking with her in the Yorkshire dales, or when we're working together to make a meal here in France. We start with the small metal box we were given as children to while away afternoons in Chesley, a box about the size of an adult hand, inside which were a variety of objects we recall only in flashes. A miniature magnifying glass, on that we agree. But what else? With the memory of the box comes the sensation of handling small hard things, although we have trouble seeing what they were. One of us will say, "A marble—I think there was a marble," and the other will cry, "Yes, yes, a marble. Wasn't it a cat's eye? Green? And weren't there buttons? Brass buttons?"

When we tire of the box we move on to the first sitting room—there were two—where there are lots of things to pick up and look at in memory. My favourite is always a brightly glazed ceramic camel, its noble head draped in tassels and its green saddlebags open, to be used for matches or toothpicks. To my dismay, after his mother's death in 1963, my father auctioned off the house and its contents, and some clever antique dealer snapped up the camel before I had a chance to rescue it. My father had no attachment to the house, perhaps because for him it was a place of great loneliness after losing his only sibling and his father. His mother eventually remarried a solid citizen named Walter Grey and in this way gave her son a good home and a university education. For this he was grateful, a dutiful son who no doubt loved his mother—all the Sunday visits, after all—but that did not mean he wanted to keep those fool knick-knacks.

My sister and I did not much love her, however, for she was not a lovable woman. Many of the lectures we received from our mother about our character defects and faults were attached to the threat of "being like Grandma." She was a difficult and prickly presence, not the kind of grandmother who'd cuddle and spoil you; she was talented, enterprising and admirable, but a hard life had made her a hard woman. Still, we love to remember what was good about her—she taught us how to bake without measuring, she played the piano with a rolling left hand and a heavy pedal, she let us put on her rouge—and we love to remember her house.

"Kitchen," Ruthie says, in the mood for some serious reminiscence. "Right hand drawer, in the sideboard."

"Balls of string, wax paper, rubber sealer rings, aluminum foil folded up in squares, pencil ends, thumbtacks in matchboxes and wooden clothes pegs. There's more, but it's your turn. Windowsill beside the kitchen settee."

"Blue-and-gold honey tins with tomato plants growing in them. And on the settee, a grey wool blanket and pillows, remember? There was one shaped like a cat, a calico cat. Oh, didn't she love her cats and her pillows!"

"Listen, I think of her every time I stuff one in behind my back in the car. She always did that, didn't she?"

"Are we talking about cats or pillows?"

Laughter, and more laughter, bringing everything with it: Grandma's pie crust, the woodstove, the slop bucket, the chiming pendulum clock, the calendar with the colour photograph of the royal princesses, the flamboyant floral wallpaper in the spare room where we slept together and there, on the lace runner of the bureau, with the tortoiseshell mirror and comb, a little china container for hair brushings. Gone, all of it.

I see from a real estate sign on the front lawn that the place has just been sold again, and I wonder if any child nowadays will lie on her stomach in the second sitting room—on winter visits, Ruthie and I would stay in there till supper, although it was cold away from the kitchen woodstove—reading all Sunday afternoon.

Much as I hated the car trip to get there, I loved my grandmother's bookshelves, the neat rows of old *Reader's Digests* and her 1918 edition of *The Books of Knowledge,* an encyclopedia for children edited by Arthur Mee. These books, all twenty of them, were the wellspring of my understanding and the source of much of my discontent. For in their pages I discovered the world, and I wanted to grow up as fast as I could and get out there and see it.

Each Volume, bound in maroon covers, was divided into various Books: "The Book of Nature," "The Book of Wonder," "The Book of Golden Deeds," "The Book of Things to Make and Do" and, most thrilling of all, "The Book of Stories." Here were condensed versions of every famous tale under the sun, combining adventure, tragedy and romance in just the right amounts to feed my imagination and to hook me into a habit that altered my life. The more I read, the more I felt myself different from those around me and the more I knew I would not, could not, stay home. It is to my father's everlasting credit that he saved those books from the auctioneer, and I have them still, today.

Leaving Chesley on my way down to Belgrave to visit my aunt, I don't bother getting the map out of the glove compartment, for I know this countryside extremely well. All I have to do is zigzag my way south on concession roads, all the while recalling that Lake Huron is to my right. I know that Belgrave is immediately south of Wingham, which is right after Teeswater on County Road 4. I know this route the way I know how to recite multiplication tables or Bible verses memorized in Sunday school, or how to play gospel hymns by ear—it's part of who I am. I take my time driving, enjoying the familiar sight of wooden barns and shiny silos, naming out loud familiar roadside flowers—Queen Anne's lace, toadflax, fireweed, chicory—and stopping now and again to drink it all in.

Eventually I reach Walkerton, and as I'm passing through remark to myself how pretty the town is and how similar to Elmira, not only in size and appearance but because both have suffered such critical problems with water supply—in Walkerton deadly E. coli from animal waste and in Elmira chemical pollution. In both cases, disaster has been the result of carelessness, blindly attendant upon progress and profit. The dreamscape of my childhood is not all it seems, for changes wrought by human beings are bringing certain peril.

Still meditating on how times are changing for the worse—clearly a sign I am turning into an old lady—I follow a lovely pattern of right/left/right down through bullrushy marshes ringed with cedar, up ridges of green pasture where rusty-coloured cattle browse, down again along fields of ripening barley and wheat. The sky is a startling shade of blue and there are no clouds. Even with these pessimistic thoughts, contemplating human folly and nature's ruin, I am amazingly happy. It is a perfect day. I see a town coming up and think I must have reached Teeswater sooner than I expected.

But the sign says Walkerton. Somehow, I have made a huge half-circle around and come back into town a different way. I pull over on the gravel shoulder and throw my head back and laugh.

"So," I say to my eyes in the rear-view mirror, "you think you know your way around, eh? Smarten up, big shot. You don't live here anymore."

HARD OF HAPPINESS

COLD BLUE SUNDAY in Latourne. There has been a
light snowfall overnight, a visible blessing on this first
winter of the new century. It will soon melt away, but
this morning the snow still lies in the vineyards across
from Mas Blanc, like alleys of silver between
untrimmed vines that bristle coppery bronze in the sun.
I go out on the terrace to discern whether the snow is
doing its usual muffle and, yes, even the birds seem
silenced. I am pleased and grateful, for I love this still-
ness, this absence of sound, this stasis. Nothing is
happening and nothing is demanded. There is nothing
to translate or understand, no one need utter a word in
exclamation or reply. There is nothing in my mind but
the pure, wordless sensation of cold and light. But even
taking pleasure in this soundlessness and the sheer,
clear absence of language, I feel the *idea* of silence

pulling others along in its wake and soon my mind crackles with the noise of words, French and English in a burning tangle, each desiring dominance.

Living here is like flying in a small plane through dense fog, every so often glimpsing the tip of a mountain or the side of a cliff, terrified by the dangers of negotiating through the murk, not knowing where I am or whether I have enough fuel to stay aloft until I get there, wherever it is I am going.

I look back at what I have written. *A simile.* One thing like another. If only I could make perfect comparisons in two languages, I'd be content/*contente*. With the right simile, I'd be able to assimilate myself and be assimilated. I am so damn tired of being taken for a good-natured nitwit, smiling ear to ear and half the time getting things wrong. If I were living in a country where I understood nothing, or couldn't speak a word, I swear it would be easier.

Funny, that I turned to the sense of sight as a way to express aural incomprehension. Not blind, not completely in the dark, but . . . uncertain. I *kind of* know what's going on, but . . . . What is worrisome is that I am so accustomed to the half-light now that I no longer demand clarity. I rather like the blur. Have I become a superficial expatriate, belonging nowhere, adept at skimming the surface and avoiding the depths?

Since coming to live in France, I have become an enthusiastic viewer of rugby on television. I love the teamwork and the action—the kicks, the throws, the scrum, the solid, muscular splat of male bodies flat up against each other, the courageous tackles and sudden brilliant runs, the perfect try when it seems that all is lost—but to tell the truth, I don't know the rules or understand the referee's hand signals. I'm just crazy about the game at its most basic, physical level. It's how I feel listening to French *chansonniers* such as Patrick Bruel: intense delight coupled with vague comprehension.

It's not as if I haven't tried to overcome my shame at nearly failing French in high school. In 1991, when we were first living in France, I studied French at Paul Valéry Université: conversation, grammar, history, politics, culture, the works. Never missed a class all year. But my life in Montpellier was led entirely in English except for the hours at school, and the French language remained foreign. Although I passed the course, the certificate merely said *Assez Bien*. Which means "good enough," to be understood by anyone competent in nuance as "not really good enough."

Living here now, a decade later, much of what I studied then has gone from mind. In order to get by, I am tuned not so much to spoken words as to expressive tone and stance, gesture and glance, shrug of shoulder, flick of wrist. All these become indicators for how I should respond in a conversation. If you are speaking French, I smile at you warmly, with convincing eye contact. I establish intimacy by standing very close and watching your mouth as it moves, my eyes never leaving your face, as if I am memorizing your every word. If I do not concentrate I will lose the thread and you will have to start again.

I have been told by my daughter that sometimes when she is speaking to me, my mouth moves in silent duplication of hers, as if I am playing "copycat," mirroring her every word. "I see you doing this with other people too," she says. "It's kind of weird, Mom. You look like an old lady."

I admit to the flaw, and wonder whether it's because I do not hear well that I am quite unconsciously copying people. I am not deaf, but I *am* a little hard of hearing. I don't think people use this expression any longer, but that's what we used to say about old Uncle Bill from Thurso, married to my mother's sister Christine, whose hearing was increasingly impaired to the point that, in his nineties, communication with him was more than hard, it was impossible. He was a dear man, smart and sweet-natured, but in his last years isolated in his own memories and given to loud monologues in lieu of actual conversation. An odd term when you think of it, *hard of hearing,* a peculiar way of saying that someone lacks the ability to hear. Why don't we say *hard of see-ing* or *hard of thinking?* Or *hard of being happy?*

Sitting in a café at Charles de Gaulle airport before seven on a rainy autumn morning, having just arrived in Paris after several weeks in Canada, I order the breakfast special—croissant, fresh orange juice, coffee. There's lots of time before my connecting plane to Montpellier, from where it will take an hour to drive to Latourne through Sommières, Quissac, Lézan . . . and then the turn to our road, and then the curve round the monastery, and the little bridge across the Ourne. . . . I am already visualizing the route, longing for the comfort of home after the tedious flight. I pull out my note-book but am too sleepy to write and spend my time looking at the other customers. Since most of them happen to be men, I am careful not to let my eyes rest too long on any individual, because even a middle-aged woman grey with fatigue and rumpled from travel is fair game for the flirtatious French, even these tired fel-lows leaning against the bar with their espresso and *petit rouge.* The last thing I want to do is to talk to any-one in this language before dawn.

I notice a young woman arriving at a table near mine. She has shoulder-length black hair and a long face with flat features I associate with people from northern Thailand or Vietnam. She's wearing large glasses low on her nose and a sad expression—through the lenses her eyes appear red and swollen. She's dressed in a dark blue jacket and jeans, with a patterned silk scarf, violet and turquoise, wound around her neck. She puts a small valise beside her and sits down in a leaden way, leaning her head on her hand and looking down at her knees. She sits like this for several minutes, her head bowed, and I see that her tears are actually making small splash marks as they fall on the table. I am moved by pity to get up and go over. I feel I have to do something, although I don't know what.

"Vous avez besoin d'aide?" I ask, bending down so I can speak softly to ask if she needs my help.

She looks up, her face wet with tears, and asks, in French, if I have a match. I go to the bar and get a small packet from the cashier and return. She has taken her cigarettes from her pocket, and when I give her the matches she asks me if I want one. I decline, and go back to my table and am just sitting down when she is at my side, her expression a mix of humiliation and hope. She says she needs a coffee.

I give her some money, thinking that maybe she just did this weeping act to get a free coffee, but when she comes back to her chair and sits down again with her cup, she looks so forlorn that I am sure she's in real distress. When she looks over again, I raise my eyebrows and turn my glance to the empty chair at my table. This is an action performed without thinking, an entirely visceral response. I do not want to talk, but I cannot bear to see her crying alone.

She tells me her name is Maguy and that she is just back from a visit to Hue in Vietnam where she was born. She has to wait until later in the morning when her mother is coming to pick her up here. She has returned with no French money, she is grateful for the coffee.

But why is she crying? Surely it has not been because of the lack of money? I do not ask this, but I say in a tone somewhere between statement and question: *"C'est évident que vous souffrez d'une grande tristesse."*

For the first time she smiles through her tears, and I assume she finds my accent amusing, although I think that what I've said is correct grammatically. *It appears that you are suffering from some great sadness.* But she is smiling, she says, because of my kindness. The word she uses is *gentillesse.*

She asks me if I want to hear why she is sad, and I tell her I have an hour before catching my flight. So she begins, partly in English—perhaps to impress me or perhaps to make it easier for me to grasp her story. She is twenty-five, a student in Paris, where she lives with a Frenchwoman, her adoptive mother. From the time of her birth she had been in an orphanage in Hue run by Roman Catholic nuns, until her mother, a single woman, came to Hue and adopted her when she was three.

Before that, when she was a baby, she had fallen from a window of the orphanage and injured her back: she remembers being in a crib and not being able to move. From the very beginning, she remembers pain. She has had many operations, but her back will never be right. Her life will never be right. Her adoptive mother has provided for her very well and loves her, but it is not enough. She has just been to visit the nuns in Hue, wanting to see if she could find her real mother, her real father, her family. Her self.

But even though she gets some information and discovers part of her history, in the long run, she says, she is no further ahead. "I do not know who I am or what I am," she says in English, tears falling now like rain. "I do not know why I exist. I feel like nothing. I many times try to kill myself. I go there to make it better, but now it is worse. I have no reason to live."

During her tale my eyes have so filled with tears that I can hardly see her across the table. I reach out and touch her hand, and say her name, Maguy. I move from the formal *vous* one uses for strangers to the intimate *tu* one uses for friends or family or, in this case appropriately, for people younger than oneself. I find myself speaking rapidly, not caring if I am making mistakes, so anxious to impress upon this young woman that she has every reason to live. I hear myself speaking in a syrupy voice (afterwards, I realize that in acting the role of benefactor, I made up a script full of clichés), insisting that she has much to give the world. That she can *use* her bitter experience in some positive way. Only if we have suffered ourselves can we truly help others, I say, and realize that I am making one of those pompous pronouncements offered by the well-meaning, as offensive and useless as "if it doesn't kill you, it'll make you stronger."

But I notice that she is not listening to what I say so much as she is absorbing my concern, my hand rubbing hers, my tears falling. We have transcended language. The hour passes, I must leave. She asks for my address, and I write it down on a piece of paper ripped from my journal, saying that I want to hear from her to be sure that she has listened to what I've said. Her face is still tear-stained, but as she smiles she's much prettier than I had first thought. We stand up and prepare to make our farewell in the French manner, the airy sideways kiss. She suddenly undoes the silk scarf and unwinds it from around her neck and holds it out to me.

"I want you to have this," she says in English. "To remember me."

I begin to demur—and then stop, for I understand that this gift *must* be given and accepted. She ties it around my neck so that it hangs loosely and, as I admire its pattern of leaves and flowers, I see that it is frayed and worn thin, that she had tied it on herself in such a way as to disguise the holes.

"*Merci,*" I say. "*Je suis très émue. Je suis très heureuse d'avoir ce souvenir de toi. Vraiment, je penserai à toi.*" Truly, I say, I am very touched and happy to have this gift. I will think of you.

We kiss, we part, I walk away and look back only once to see her waving goodbye.

Within the week there is a card from her, to which I respond. At Christmas, there is a box of chocolates and, most touching of all, a letter from her mother inviting me to visit if ever I am in Paris. Maguy has not been entirely well, but she has not tried to commit suicide since coming back from Hue, she says.

Some years have passed now, our cards back and forth are less frequent; and although I travel often, I have not stopped in Paris on any of my trips. I always just pass through Charles de Gaulle and make my connections. You'd think that someone living only an hour away by plane—just three hours by TGV train— would go up to Paris simply for pleasure. Well, maybe this year. Maybe this year I will go to visit Maguy.

A week after meeting Maguy, I was travelling again, but this time by train, necessitating an hour's car journey southeast to Nîmes to make a direct connection to Geneva, and an international writing conference. I'd been asked to bring some of my books to sell and was taking one box in a large sisal bag and the rest in a small valise. I was also carrying a briefcase, my overnight suitcase and a purse over my shoulder. I managed everything from the car into the Nîmes station but, at the bottom of the escalator, *panique!* I couldn't get both myself and my baggage on the moving steps at the same time, and people were lining up behind, muttering angrily. I could hear a man shouting *"Allons-y!"* but the more I tried to balance the bags, the more overwrought and clumsy I became, cursing myself for being so vain as to bring so many books. It could have been funny had the crowd not been growing in size and noise.

"Vous avez besoin d'aide?"

I looked round to see an attractive woman, with grey hair arranged softly around her face, smiling sympathetically and putting out a hand to take one of my bags. I grinned in gratitude and passed her the one full of books, heavy as sin but at least with a good leather strap. I got the other bags up and on and regained a little composure. When we reached the top and boarded the train, she turned out to be in the same car as I was, and together we lifted my suitcase and books onto the luggage rack at the door. I told her that she was very kind and headed for my reserved seat at the far end.

She was sitting on her own halfway along when I passed on my way to get a bottle of Perrier, and we nodded and smiled as if we knew each other. I saw that she was reading and correcting what appeared to be a manuscript and wondered if perhaps she was going to the same conference: it was entirely possible, as there were writers expected from several European countries.

On the way back to my seat I asked, in English, if this was the case. She replied, in English, that no, this was a Buddhist text she was correcting for a friend. She invited me to sit down, said her name was Simone and that she was on her way to visit a married daughter outside Geneva. She was happy to talk in English, explaining that not only had she, in Swiss fashion, studied several languages at school, she had also spent a year in San Francisco learning a special caregiving technique at a clinic for AIDS patients.

In the intimate way of strangers on trains, we unwound the stories of our lives. She told me that she is an artist, and that her French husband is an architect. They live only half an hour from Latourne in a village near Uzès, famous for its Renaissance towers—visible on the skyline from a great distance—and the colourful abundance of its Saturday markets. As Simone described how she uses her particular care-giving skills at a home for the aged in Uzès, I understood that the town's beauty and charm have nothing to do with her reality. She volunteers to spend time with the sick and the dying because it is something she has to do, she said, to balance artistic isolation and self-centredness.

The technique, as she described it, is simple. "Allow people to have their pain," she said. "Do not try to change what they are feeling."

At first, I was incredulous. Surely she did not mean disallowing analgesics, relaxants, morphine? No, she did not mean that. She meant that individuals must be left with the dignity of their own experience, whatever it might be. She meant that interference in someone else's distress, even when done with good intentions, can have a harmful, neutralizing effect on the fragile ego. "The best thing we can give people is a safe place where they can be themselves, free from our desire to change them. We can restore equilibrium by our total acceptance."

I admitted to belonging in the damnable class of those who attempt to alter what people are feeling. ("Don't be sad," I said to Maguy. "Darling, try to be happy," I say to my daughter. "Be grateful for what you have and stop moaning," I scold myself.) It seemed to me, as Simone's calm and reasonable explanation continued, that she had brought me information I needed to hear, a kind of mental halter to hold me back a bit from my usual desire to fix everything. Silence, she said, can often be more powerful than words.

We were still talking when we arrived at Geneva, but before we parted company we exchanged telephone numbers, promising to meet again. After Christmas I invited her and her husband for lunch, and it seemed that we established some foundation of common interests for an ongoing friendship, although, as he spoke no English, our conversation did not seem as deep and intensely fulfilling as it had on the train.

At Simone's urging, a few weeks later I attended an afternoon meeting of caregivers outside Uzès, a group being instructed in Buddhist meditation techniques by a disciple of Sogyal Rinpoche, whose low, pleasant voice led us through a series of exercises, some of them solitary but most of them for two or three people working together, sharing each other's intimate thoughts and feelings. But, of course, *tout en français*. As it happened, at the last minute Simone was unable to attend and, although the group was welcoming and warm, I felt shy and out of place. Uncertain whether I correctly understood the woman's directions, I couldn't clear my mind to meditate. I never went again; it seemed *inutile*.

We saw each other at the Uzès market one Saturday morning in the spring, Simone and I, as we were buffeted by crowds around us at a fruit stall. We embraced, we talked briefly, we promised to get together. "I'll call," we both said at once, and laughed merrily.

But we have not. Time passes, and our lives veer off in directions that do not include each other. I do not feel rejected, nor do I feel guilty for not calling. She gave what she had to give, and I learned what I needed to know. We made a perfect transaction, in the past tense.

Mid-January, Thursday morning, market day in near-by Anduze, and I go with Bob to make the usual rounds: weekly bunch of tulips, three kinds of olives and two kinds of cheese, bread, fresh vegetables and a dozen clementines. As my face is now familiar to the merchants and farmers, at every stall we exchange a few words as I am taking out my change purse and counting coins. Weather is the topic we normally choose, but today it's the euro—getting used to the new money, prices being altered upward, problems with vending machines—we are all delighted with the euro as a conversational gambit, whether or not we are pleased with the currency itself.

Today, besides doing the shopping, I am accompanying Bob to a small *salon de coiffure* near the bridge; there's a sign in the window giving prices for both men and women. We've looked in and have decided we like the sensible appearance of the middle-aged woman whose shop it seems to be. She looks like someone who will listen and not just do whatever she wants. Bob, who has thinning hair, wants a light trim, a *coupe d'entretien:* the problem lies in the interpretation of *coupe* for, after his last visit to a hairdressing shop around the corner, he had almost no hair left because he didn't know he should have asked for layering:

coupe en dégradé. The term always makes me think of someone humbling hair by degrading it, stomping on it with dirty boots and calling it vile names. Nevertheless, as I now understand exactly what must be said, I have offered to speak to the *coiffeuse,* woman to woman, to make sure that this cut will be done correctly.

As I expected, she smiles when I say I have brought my little boy to have his hair cut, but she understands exactly how the layering should be done and invites me to sit down and wait, as the cut will take only a few minutes. She is a friendly soul and, having noted our accents, she comments that there are many English people living in the area now. We feel compelled to explain that no, we are actually Canadian and Scottish. I ask her if she is from the region and she says she grew up in Paris but has been here for twenty years. And then she goes on to tell us that, in fact, her father was also Scottish. And her mother English.

"But then you speak English!" I exclaim, wondering why she didn't say so earlier. Maybe she finds our efforts funny?

"Mais, non," she says, *"pas du tout. C'est bizarre, mais . . . c'est vrai."* Strange but true, she says, she speaks not a word. And the reason is even stranger, she says, as she puts down her scissors in order to tell the tale.

When she was very young, just a baby, her older sister fell ill with some kind of brain disease. She says she thinks it must have been meningitis, but at the time all her parents knew was that the child's brain had been terribly affected by something invisible and that this had resulted in her death. The family doctor had an entirely reasonable explanation for the tragedy: the girl's mind, he declared, had been severely damaged through speaking English with her parents. She had been forced to think in two languages, and the result was cerebral fatigue. Furthermore, it seemed to him that the parents had only themselves to blame. Poor child!

And so, the hairdresser continues, as she goes back to cutting Bob's hair, her mother never again spoke to her in English. Never again would she take chances with her family's health. She forbade her husband to speak English as well, to ensure that the remaining daughter would not fall prey to the fatal consequences of linguistic confusion. And she made her daughter promise to speak only French, forever.

I am full of questions, but politeness dictates that I not ask them all at once. Instead, I say I will come soon for a trim myself, hoping that then I may discover the rest of the story. What were the Scot and the Englishwoman doing in Paris, and how had they learned to speak a second language so well that they could live in it? How could they have believed the dreadful doctor? Did they not wonder that speaking two languages had not destroyed *their* brains? Why didn't they flee back to the land of their maternal tongue? Did they not consider that perhaps it was not the surfeit of English words in their child's head that had killed her, but the French?

Bob and I chew at this story as soon as we are out of the shop—she has degraded his hair to perfection—savouring the delicious taste of something really strange. We walk through the winding streets to the café, Le Petit Jardin, where Jean-Claude will bring us our usual *café crème* and we'll read the papers before going home. The parents must have been simple people, we decide, and the doctor some kind of elderly quack.

"But look here," I say, "French *does* give me a headache. Maybe we're playing with fire, you know? Maybe we should leave while we still can and go back home." I am laughing as I say this, joking around the way I do, and of course I don't really mean it. Yet oddly enough, I can feel tears on my face and, as we enter the café and greet Jean-Claude with the obligatory handshake, he notices my wet cheeks and asks if I am sad about something: *"Vous êtes triste, madame?"*

"No, no," I say. "It's this awful winter wind. It always makes my nose run and my eyes water and it seems unusually bitter today." I take some tissues from my bag to wipe my face, inelegantly blowing my nose to prove my point. I feel my husband's gaze upon me, apprehensive and tender.

"Tell me, Jean-Claude," I say then. "You know these things. Tell me which one it is today, the

Tramontane from the Pyrénées, or the *Mistral* that blows down the Rhône? If I am going to live here, I must learn to distinguish the winds."

FIRE

Spring Fire

ALL DAY WE WORK in the olive grove, pruning the trees so that their boughs will spread like grey-green wings and bear fruit in the fall. We have learned how to do the pruning from observing a demonstration at the *Fête des Oliviers* in nearby Alès, and we know that we must be ruthless, leaving space enough in the centre of each tree "for a dove to fly through." We are to cut off everything vertical: all these tender new twigs shooting up from the branches must be chopped. We must shape the olive tree to our needs, bending it to our will with our knives and clippers. We do not want leaves, we want olives, and we want them close to the ground and easy to pick. We have understood all this in theory— and in French, too—and now we are putting it into practice. There are only fourteen trees, some probably planted not more than ten or twelve years ago, but others are many decades older than that, gnarled and hollow survivors of the killing freeze of 1956.

In one corner of the grove we are burning dead wood left from last autumn's clearing of bushes along the roadside, and we keep a small fire going all afternoon, throwing freshly cut branches on the flames from time to time, relishing the glorious oily sizzle and crackle. The old wood gives off a sweet white smoke like steam, but the olive burns black and greasy, and there's a roaring sound deep in the blaze that grows during the afternoon. It seems that something savage dwells in the heart of the fire, and I think I'd better get water "just in case." It is an absurd waste of time— what few sparks there are fall onto damp grass—but nevertheless I carry two plastic buckets down to the Ourne, a field away from where we are working.

After making my way through a tangle of brambles, I bend down at a riverbank lush with violets and wild narcissus and see myself reflected in the still water just before I dip the pail. I have the vivid impression of having done this before, if not in life, then in a dream. Hauling the water back through wild iris and blackthorn, I stop to look up at the poplars on the other bank, their new leaves glimmering pale copper against the deep blue sky. *I am part of this place.* The phrase comes like a prayer of gratitude—although I do not

directly say thank you to anyone or anything. Twice, I
make a circle of water around the fire so that it cannot
spread. I feel as if I am doing some slow ritual Dance
of the Elements, its movements dictated by centuries of
tradition. I am laughing because I know what I am
doing is silly, but I persist.

How many times over the years have friends
declared, in tones of exasperation as often as affection,
that I am a Romantic? And how many times have I
agreed and said that I've always known I was born in
the wrong century, I should have run with Wordsworth
and Coleridge and that whole crowd. Instead, here I
am, skirting along the poetic hem of pantheism, wanting to be drawn in but too modern to submit. Yet it
seems, this day, that I am having not only a slightly
comic revelatory moment but am also seeing several
layers of experience at once—connecting myself to the
natural world in just the way old Wordsworth might
have approved.

I step back and look out as if I am watching someone else. I see a man and woman cutting branches and
twigs off olive trees. He is wearing a denim jacket he
has had for thirty years, the collar badly frayed. She is
wearing a faded brick-red cotton shirt and a patterned
silk scarf around her hair. It is a sunny afternoon, and
the grass under the trees is an aching, brilliant green.
I see the fire and the smoke, and the way the flames
leap up, and I watch the woman go to the stream for

water and then pour it, swinging the pail in a rhythmic way. She seems to be doing a daft little dance around the fire.

The two people I see are part of a long chain of human beings cultivating the earth. They are also part of their own careful braiding of event and memory, this day another link in the long story they tell themselves about days they have spent together working outdoors. They have an easy relationship with each other and the land, possible only for those who have never been true farmers. Although there were years when they were dependent on their garden for what food they ate, they are at a point in their lives now when they can buy everything they need at the market. Cultivating olive trees is, in the final analysis, for the novelty of picking olives in December and taking them to the mill to have a little oil made for their own use.

But in their gestures and their movements, these two people are doing the same work as the French farmers around them, whose activities are not a copy but real labour-for-money without which they cannot exist. Nevertheless, even if the couple in the grove are not genuine peasants, the effort of this pruning is real enough—the blister on the inside of my thumb a painful reminder to wear gloves right from the start, the ache in my arms from wielding the big clippers bone-deep. When we are done at the end of the day I am glad to take one last pail and splash it on the smouldering ashes before walking through the field to the house, a bath, a book, a glass of wine.

Summer Fire

Two years after we married in Toronto, we moved to Belleville, a pretty town of thirty-five thousand, on Lake Ontario across from the Isle of Quinte. We bought a century-old brick house on Marshall Road, only half a kilometre outside the town limits but, at that point in the early 1970s, still "in the country" with open fields and a swamp behind us. A plain, flat-faced house without architectural charm, it had several lovely old maples lining one side of the drive, and an adjacent hectare of property so that we had, for the seven years we lived there, an enormous garden. Although we did not fit into the authentic "back to the land" category because we both had jobs—Bob taught at the community college and I worked at the daily paper—our lives revolved around our garden. During the winter months, with seed catalogues and graph paper on which to plot the rows, we planned; in the spring we planted, in the summer we weeded and harvested, and then froze and pickled and jellied until we were glad for autumn frosts that killed off whatever was left. We grew corn and zucchini and radishes, Jerusalem artichokes and green and yellow beans, peas and carrots and cabbage, potatoes and beets and chard, lettuce and cucumber and eggplant, tomatoes and onions and herbs: rosemary, thyme, parsley, sage, lemon balm and mint. We planted asparagus our first spring and within three years were feeding friends and neighbours as well as ourselves.

We inherited rhubarb and a tangle of grapevines, a thicket of raspberries and a large overgrown strawberry patch in decline, although it did well enough for a few years to let us make jam and a gallon of rosé wine. We made wine from the rhubarb too, and from the blue concord grapes, and from the thousands of dandelions crowding out the grass in our so-called front lawn. We saw ourselves existing happily in symbiosis with those bright yellow flowers: we gave them space and they gave us pleasure. The wine we made was symbolic of how we lived on Marshall Road: those were years when we had little money but much enthusiasm, years of companion planting and organic mulching and marigolds everywhere to banish the nematodes. We thought we'd be there forever and on the lawn beside the house planted several fruit trees under which I imagined we might someday see grandchildren frolic.

Somewhere, I must still have our recipe for that weedy wine, but I have no inclination to make it again, knowing full well how much time and effort is involved. The process began in late spring, when we would gather dandelion heads over a weekend, plucking the

yellow petals free of their bitter milky calyx and dump-
ing them into a plastic garbage can with water and
sugar and yeast and bananas, the "secret ingredient"
for creating a smooth dry wine. Now, nearly three
decades later, in my mind's eye I can see us crouching
down in the damp, low-ceilinged cellar, siphoning liquid from one container to another, and then later into a
ten-gallon glass carboy where it would continue to fer-
ment, bubbling its way to a state we would pronounce
"done" several months later, when we'd bottle it.
Usually, we'd find some special occasion to open the first
bottle, such as an unexpected March snowfall, which
would accentuate our delight in the wine's sharp dry
taste—summer in the mouth. We'd hold our glasses to
the light to admire the clarity and beauty of the pale
golden wine, and then raise them in a toast to the fertil-
ity of that front lawn and our refusal to use 2, 4-D.

We became quite famous among our friends for our
dandelion wine, as it was not only surprisingly delicious but potent. Strong men would topple after a third
glass if they hadn't learned to pace themselves and eat
a great deal at the same time. And oh, we did eat. In the
cellar we had an ancient two-section Dominion freezer
that had come with the house, as big as a coffin and
twice as deep. (During that time, as part of a community outreach program, I taught an evening course in
English at Warkworth Penitentiary, about an hour's
drive away. One of the inmates, a good-looking and

nicely mannered man, was said to have been incarcer-
ated for having chopped up his wife and hidden her in
the family freezer. It was not often that I went down to
get something to thaw for supper that I did not think of
that man. Or of his wife.) We filled the smaller section
with meat—we'd buy a side of beef and a side of
pork—and crammed the other with all the freezable
vegetables we picked from the garden, plus containers
of sour cherries we bought every year from orchards in
nearby Prince Edward County.

I learned everything about gardens and cooking
from books or from new friends around Belleville
who were leading similar lives. Although my mother
had grown up on a farm, women of her generation
had left their rural pasts behind and had scant interest
in time-wasting chores such as making their own
breads or soups. This is not *strictly* true, as every
September my mother and her best friend Dot put
down pickles and chili sauce, but those were condi-
ments, meant to enhance meals, not the stuff of life
itself. I grew up as did many others in the 1950s, on
canned soup and cake mixes: there was no shame for
our up-to-date mothers in serving instant foods like
Kraft Dinner. And so there I was at age thirty, married
to a Scot from Edinburgh who knew no more about
any of it than I did, and we had no choice but to
plunge in together, cookbooks and garden manuals
and *Harrowsmith* magazine in hand.

There's a photo of us from the early 1970s that shows us as we were. I have chubby cheeks and long wheat-coloured braids, and am wearing a get-up that must have been my do-it-yourself notion of the peasant look: loose overblouse, long skirt, heavy boots, the whole kit. Bob is wearing denim—the same jacket he wears in the olive grove—and his beard is long and shaggy. It is hard to imagine we didn't know how ludicrous we must have appeared to the good burghers of Belleville, but our faces glow with such earnest virtue that, to my eye now, we look adorable.

Our place in the country quickly became an attractive retreat for friends from Toronto, providing as we did the ambiance of "the rural weekend" particularly in late summer, when a visit might also involve swimming in Lake Ontario, or fishing on the Skootamatta that winds its rivery way through forests north of Tweed. Entertaining guests was easy—simply a matter of exploring the back roads of Hastings County with our canoe tied on top of the car and our bathing suits at the ready. And then, at the end of the day, back at the house on Marshall Road, there'd be a meal outside on the edge of the garden where we'd made a trestle table out of an old door and fashioned a ring of stones for a small firepit. Someone would bring out kindling and logs from our woodshed and get a blaze going, while the rest of us picked what we wanted to cook—corn, potatoes, carrots, beets,

beans, cabbage—or tomatoes and radishes and lettuce to eat raw.

Once the fire was ready, a huge open kettle of water
would be set to boil while we washed the vegetables
under the pump by the side of the house—a two-
person job, one to wash and one to crank the handle up
and down. For some people this is the moment they
remember, scrubbing the potatoes under the flush of
cold well water before eating. For most of our friends,
however, their memories focus on lifting their food
from the boiling water—everything dyed pink if we'd
included beets—and slathering it with butter before
chewing and swallowing in what was a kind of holy
silence. There'd be very little conversation, just mur-
murs of gustatory appreciation and occasional exclamations about how *alive* this food seemed to the palate,
how the taste was utterly different from vegetables
purchased in the city.

With the meal there'd be pickles and chili sauce set
out on the table, and homemade bread with cheese and
butter from Riverside Dairy down the road, and as
many bottles of wine as seemed necessary. Slowly the
pot on the fire would be emptied, slowly everyone
would moan with satisfaction and go off to take a stroll
around the garden or down to the front lawn for a final
game of crazy candlelit croquet. Later, when the dishes
were done and the stars were out, we'd build up the
fire and sit around watching the bats flitter and dance

overhead. If there were children along, there'd be marshmallows to roast, and if there were only adults, then sweet wine and coffee. We'd sit there talking until the fire had burned down to glowing coals, until the chill of the night made our backs shiver, until there were no words left and there was only silence in between the creaking of the crickets and the croaking of the frogs.

Autumn Fire

Late November afternoon, the air cold and damp, the sky heavy and sullen with dull grey clouds, the entire world seems in a rotten mood. I am cranky and low-spirited myself—tired, and my left elbow is aching again. All very well to have the benevolent shade of the *micocoulier* tree in the summer, but in autumn its fallen leaves blanket the driveway and path beside the house, and the terrace needs to be swept off daily. There are far too many leaves for the compost, and so I take several loads in the wheelbarrow down to the bottom of our property near the stream. When I've made a pretty good pile I light a roll of newspaper and stick it deep in the centre of the leaves and the fire begins with huge drifts of white smoke. Now the work of raking takes on some meaning, and my efforts quicken as I gather armfuls of leaves to keep feeding the fire.

As the afternoon darkens, I work with such determination that I forget my aches and pains, trying to get these leaves burned before the leaden clouds bring rain. The smoke is pale and fragrant, but it does not smell like maple leaves burning in my childhood; nevertheless, it is enough to stir memories and to give me energy to finish the job before nightfall.

Who reading this is old enough to remember a time when people burned autumn leaves? Before we knew it was *wrong*, before we knew about carbon pollution and greenhouse gases and global warming, before there were municipal orders to pack dead leaves into plastic bags for garbage pickup. I remember, and memory gives me the same scene every time: King Street, a maple-lined residential street running through Elmira from the Cenotaph at one side of town and connecting with Highway 86 at the other. All along the street on October Saturdays, most families would have bonfires out by the curb, being tended by dads, while moms raked up leaves into heaps and kids were running everywhere, chasing each other through the piles and leaping over the fires. In memory, my friend Sally and I are always twelve years old, riding our bicycles down King Street, wheeling our way in lazy sweeping figure eights around the fires on either side of the street, clouds of pale smoke making our eyes water but filling our noses and lungs with an agreeable perfume. Only a few years later we will take up smoking, swiping our mothers' du Mauriers and hiding in cellars and attics for a quick puff after school, just for the hell of it.

I am burning leaves all these decades later, feeling a bit guilty and furtive even though I will use the ashes to improve the soil organically, in the garden and around the olive trees. Besides, there are no edicts against it here—rubbish fires are common in this countryside, where vine trimmings are regularly burned along with every sort of inflammable debris. At all times of the year, except summer when it is too dry and dangerous, blue plumes rise from vineyards and villages and drift like ghosts over the hills. Haddou and his family, in the back section of Mas Blanc, often have fires in their yard, uncultivated land at the far end of their long garden that runs parallel with the stream and this house.

That yard. Every time I look over there I feel a wave of irritation followed by a wash of shame for having such cross thoughts. But the truth is, I wish they kept their yard tidier. I hate to admit it, but I can't help *noticing* those rolls of wire fencing and an old caravan trailer and a plastic rowboat and hoses and pipes and pots and pails and sheets of rusting metal and stacks of unidentifiable, broken things for which a use might someday be found (although one can only doubt it), and a ramshackle chicken coop that also shelters geese and ducks and rabbits and, occasionally, a goat. It is not a pretty sight.

I know, I know. It's rural France. Bruno, the neighbour whose part of the Mas is directly next to ours, teases me and mocks my attempts to prettify our section with Provençal-blue shutters on the windows and pots of geraniums along the wall—and, at the bottom of the stone stairs, our Bul-ul flowerpots from the Philippines giving the place an exotic air not at all Cévenol.

"Ce n'est pas la banlieue," he says, reminding me I am not in the suburbs, I am deep in the country where people have more to do than straightening their yards and where neatness is not a virtue. The area around his house is as jubilantly laissez-faire as Haddou's—Bruno is not interested in appearances and does not allow himself to get bogged down by bourgeois values. Besides, he is convinced that burglars are only attracted to prosperous-looking properties, and by not engaging in visible home improvements he saves himself the worry of being robbed. My bedroom window faces his side of Mas Blanc, and as I open the curtains each morning there is opportunity to look downward upon his clever system for foiling thieves. Over time my affection for Bruno has taught me to lift my eyes unto the hills.

It could well be that my impatience about a relaxed style of yard maintenance has increased as my relationship with Haddou's family has diminished. No longer do I sit at their round table sipping sweet mint tea as we watch Moroccan television (their satellite dish is turned to North Africa and ours picks up German stations, make of that what you will). Those days seem to be over, and the reasons are as complex as our dissimilar cultures, languages and ages. Now that Sonya and Saphira, the teenage daughters with whom I had the most contact, are working in cafés in Anduze and have pretty well left home, now that Hassan the elder son is no longer interested in doing garden chores for pocket money, there is little to bring us together. As the family have their own access road around the vineyards and need not pass by the front of Mas Blanc, we can go for days without seeing one another, unless we are working in the garden at the same time—in which case, the smiling, decisive head nod and a called-out greeting have replaced long conversations. The novelty of exploring each others' differences has passed.

We do see the youngest children, Hakim and Leila, as they play by the stream and ride their bikes up and down our lane, and sometimes they come around to ask for a donation to the school lotto or to show their new kittens. Leila came for help with English homework for a while, but her interest soon waned, or perhaps I did not make the lessons enough fun. Although our lives continue to be intertwined with Haddou's in a balanced, neighbourly way—we give him a bag of seed potatoes, he helps us plow our land—it is clear that the first blaze of fascination has burned down to embers.

I stand with my rake and feel the night coming down dark and mean as I consider my intolerance for a little honest mess. A cleansing fire of the spirit, that's what I need.

Winter Fire

Surprisingly cold for this time of year, says Yvonne, the village postmistress. I saw her this morning and, as usual when I go in to post a letter, we have a conversation about the weather, a topic for which I am developing an elaborate vocabulary, thanks to Yvonne. She keeps track of temperatures and rainfall in a little notebook, her dates and figures written in perfect columns in a small, neat hand. She says that she hasn't had time to check her records, but doesn't remember it ever being so frigid this early in December. We had a light snowfall a few days ago, a mere sprinkle, but it has stayed on the ground, and that's *very* unusual, she says, frowning in a manner that forecasts more terrible surprises to come. We shake our heads in mutual dismay and agree that we are shocked by yet another proof of how unreliable the weather is nowadays. What can one do? We shrug and smile and turn to other matters.

Later in the day I get myself set up in front of the fireplace, where I've had a fire going since early morning to warm the house. Although my study upstairs is comfortable enough, there's something cheerier about working in the living room on a cold and dreary day, sitting by the fire in my great-grandmother's rocking chair to read. I'm sorting two boxes of journals and letters and photographs brought down from the attic, material I've not looked at for years but have carted around from country to country in cardboard containers on which is scrawled *private papers*. I've hit a place in my work where I need to get the past more firmly in mind—nostalgia, after all, cannot sustain itself without being fed. I empty one box onto the low table beside me and out of a thin green journal, labelled 1979–80, falls a dry strip of newsprint: I can tell by the typeface it was clipped from *The Globe and Mail*.

ROSE LEFT IN MAILBOX, WOMAN DIES IN CAR FIRE
Shortly before 6:28 a.m. yesterday, a 37-year-old woman placed a single rose in the mailbox of a T_____ firm. She then went back to a green Pontiac Firebird parked in front of the R_____ company. The firm's president, Mr. P_____ is the owner of the 1968 Firebird. Inside the car, gasoline-soaked newspapers filled the back seat and the passenger side of the front seat. The woman rolled up the windows and locked the door. At 6:28 a.m. the Fire Department was called. Despite the intense heat and flames, the car's horn was still blowing, Deputy Chief S_____ said. So Captain M_____ put his hand

through the window—the heat had caused it to blow out— to pull the hood release in order to disconnect the battery. "That's when he saw the body. They didn't know anyone was in the car until then. Her body was completely burned."

Good God. Did I save this because I thought it was material I might use for fiction? No, clearly it is a kind of poem, I can see just how I could rearrange the line breaks to make it *look* like one. Is that why I kept it?

More than two decades have passed since I clipped this story from the newspaper, and I am shaken, reading it again, but I do what I always do when I am alarmed: step back and do the old heart-mind split. Intellectualize the experience, look for the archetypal aspects, locate the underlying mythic elements. If I call this tragic event *the death of a poet,* that may make it bearable to think about.

Certainly, the woman—I am convinced her name was Rose—had a poet's romantic attachment to imagery as well as a profound sense of eponymous metaphor. She performed her self-destruction as carefully as if she were writing a sonnet, she planned it with an extraordinary grasp of simile, and she accomplished an act of revenge dense with allusion and symbolism.

Slipping into the role of Teacher, leading myself through interpretative analysis in preparation for a lesson, I begin to feel less distressed. Armed with academic paraphernalia, one can more easily face the horrors and stare them down. Even though I am no longer in the classroom, I persist in the fond belief that if life can be explained and dealt with, it can be borne. Even footnoted.

I think that I might use this news item after all, not for my own writing but for the next fiction workshop I give in the spring, for novice writers of short stories. I start making notes on how to proceed. I will read aloud the news item and begin: *What are the first questions a good reporter asks?* One of them will tell me—there's bound to be an ex-journalist in a fiction workshop— *Who, Where, What, When, Why and How.*

But, I'll say, fiction writers don't necessarily need to ask questions about fact: we fill gaps by making conjectures. Out of what is *not* given here, out of the spaces and silences, we can fashion a story. For example, we might invent a failed love affair between Rose and the owner of the Firebird—a bit facile, but one needs to start somewhere. We might assume he's married and that Rose has been his little number on the side. . . . Only speculation, but there's something so compelling about this suicide that even our assumptions take on the hue of melodrama. The trick now is to crosscut these first impulses with something else, I'll say. Imagine the easiest possibilities, and then move sideways and under and around the material. What else might you fabricate? What other stories might suggest themselves?

Perhaps I will give them an exercise: *Write four pages of dialogue representing the final conversation between the owner of the car and Rose.* There'll be someone who can't imagine it, and my advice will be to conceive of a quarrel, in which the nature of the relationship shows itself and illuminates this woman's motivation. What happened to Rose so that she mixed up such a lethal cocktail of hate and love? Might she have been pregnant and might he have suggested that she "get rid of it"? Or did he refuse, when she asked him to get in the car and drive off with her to start a new life? Close your eyes and listen, I'll say, until you can hear their voices.

Where's the story here? That's what I will ask them to consider. *The Globe and Mail* decided that what was interesting about this material was the timing. The rose placed in the mailbox, the car door shut and the match lit and the burning body falling forward on the wheel, the horn beginning to blow and someone hearing the noise, looking out the window, seeing the car afire, calling the firemen. Is this what we think is important?

And then I'll give these new writers my point of view—not mine in any original sense, but absorbed over the years from others—that a good short story is not about what happens, but about the individuals to whom it happens. Not the action per se, but the people whose lives are changed, in whatever way. Perhaps the real story resides with the man who is left with guilt and grief and a ruined car. Or maybe that man's wife. Or Rose's mother—let's think about *her*, poor soul. What about the Captain? Imagine him young and new to the job and see how he reaches into the smouldering car and touches the charred body. Imagine being the Captain whose life changes.

Imagine being Rose.

Oh, that Rose. She was always so volatile.

No, now look, it's not funny, this is not the place for cynical humour. There *are* rules, after all, even for writers. This is about death and a wicked act of violence intended to harm others. Suicide *is* a kind of terrorism, isn't it? Intimidation and incrimination from beyond the grave.

I sit by this glowing fire, my plans for the afternoon rearranged by the chance discovery of this Firebird tale. I can think of nothing else; I am in its thrall, my brain filling with red roses and the acrid smell of smoke. What is most striking about what I have just read, I decide, are the visual images. I can *see* the flaming metal carapace in which the burned body folds over into ash. I begin to doubt if a story is up to the task of describing these images. A film is what is needed, not words on paper. *A film*. Before my eyes, as if I were sitting in the darkened cinema, the scenes begin. I am not sure how we will arrive at Rose's final moment and whether, indeed, that will *be* the final moment. But I am sure there will be snow falling when the car goes up in flames. I can see it, fire and ice. It must be done subtly, just a light snowfall, a few gentle flakes. . . .

All of a sudden I am disgusted by my morbidity and by the idea of preying on the lives—or deaths—of strangers. I get up and walk around the room, noticing how chilly it seems as soon as I leave the fire. Is this where writing has led me? Not for one heartless moment have I considered the *real* people involved. They've been nothing but ideas for a writing lesson.

I take the little piece of newsprint and crumple it before tossing it in the fireplace, where it turns to ash in no time at all. I sit back down, ready to start again with the journals. But the words I've read—though they no longer exist, though they are nothing but ash to be carried out in a bucket tomorrow morning and scattered around the olive trees—those words have written themselves into my head from where they can be retrieved, endlessly. And I bow to the power of language and am ashamed, for I know that now you have read this, and I have passed the story on.

I did some further research in *The Globe and Mail* archives when I decided to reproduce the story here, and discovered that the dead woman's name was not Rose, nor was she the Firebird owner's girlfriend. She was his estranged wife, despondent over their divorce proceedings. The event took place at the end of March and the death notice in early April says "Suddenly" . . . and that the woman was cremated. The weather was warm, 14°C, and there was no snow.

SNOW

Yesterday we had a snowstorm that lasted from early morning right on through the night, and now the world is clothed in white. Snowfall this heavy is rare, here on the lower edge of the Cévennes, where the foothills begin rolling up out of the vineyards. Farther north and into the mountains, there's always enough to ensure winter skiing but in Latourne, if it comes at all, it's only a light teasing tickle, a mere frosting. Today's snow, however, is thick and deep and means to stay. *This* snow would do Ottawa proud.

Shortly before dawn this morning—the sky still dark—the telephone rings, and a gruff male voice informs me that he is the courier service and has a package to deliver, and where is my house. He is calling on his cellphone from the *mairie* on the main road, and he needs directions. I explain—I've memorized this patter in French—and when I get to the bit about his turning the corner around the monastery and continuing over the small bridge, he stops me.

He says he will not be able to come to my house, for not only are the narrow country roads leading to Mas Blanc blocked with snow, but he will not attempt to cross the bridge. He understands now where I am located, and he knows that little bridge: it has no railing. Under the snow, the roads are sheer ice, he says, he could slide off. He will not do it. Don't I know that overnight everything has been freezing? It's too dangerous, *madame*, he says.

My stars, I say to myself, what a wimpy courier. But I do know that he has reason to be fearful, as I was out in the blizzard yesterday and saw for myself that cars were slipping and sliding out of control, several in accidents and even more headfirst in ditches along the highway. Of course, given the unlikelihood of this kind of weather, no one has snow tires, and there are no plows or machines to scatter sand and salt: one simply manages as best one can and waits for the snow to melt and disappear, which, ordinarily, it will do within hours.

Thus I am understanding and polite, and when he asks if I will come over to meet him, if he drives as far as the old church of St-Baudile across the way, I agree. It never occurs to me, I realize later, that I might ask *him* to walk to my house. No, and he wouldn't have done it, either.

I throw on clothes over my flannel pyjamas and pull on a pair of old winter boots I smartly brought back last summer from the attic where they'd been stored in Ottawa since I left in 1987. As soon as I step out the door and smell the silvery fragrance of new snow, I realize that this call has been a gift from the gods, for without it I would never have ventured out so early and would have missed this odd sensation of being enveloped in pastel light, as if I am dancing through a dream sequence in an old Hollywood musical. The rising sun, filtered through pearly clouds and reflected by the snow, shines everywhere. The eastern sky is rose grey streaked with lemony gold, and the vineyards are glowing blue and apricot. The world has turned, overnight, into an opal.

The birds are already at their feeder under the *mico-coulier* tree, making busy little *"dix-huit, dix-huit"* noises, but as I walk farther down the lane I hear nothing and am struck by the solemn and ponderous nature of snow itself, the grave way it stifles sound. The silence feels like a secret I cannot tell.

As I walk across the narrow bridge and around the monastery, I see that the courier has been right, for the road is really quite icy under the snow, and he would easily have gone off into the stream that still runs merrily, not yet frozen over. I make my way through the vineyard instead of the road to reach the church, where I can see there's a small blue van parked and waiting. Inside sits the courier, a red-faced man about my age, who has been watching me scuff through the snow. I am wearing my old rabbit-fur hat held on by a plaid scarf, and he probably finds me pretty funny, for I see that he is laughing.

He gets out to give me the package—I have to sign for it—and we exchange a few pleasantries about the weather. I tell him I am Canadian and this is nothing, *monsieur,* really nothing, compared with what one encounters in Ottawa. If one has the correct tires, one can drive in snow like this with no problem, I say, but of course here. . . . I shrug meaningfully and let the sentence dangle, sharp criticism of France—and all things French—implied.

He laughs again and drives off, and I walk home with the sun, now fully up from behind the clouds, making everything ahead of me glitter and gleam. I feel a great ball of joy welling up in my throat, a balloon of laughter ready to float out into the bright air. White snow lies luminous everywhere and the package in my hands, I can see from the address, is from a Canadian publisher. Too curious to wait, I stop and tear open the end of the padded envelope and pull out a letter telling me that, at the author's request, I have been sent these galleys of her new novel, *A Student of Weather.* Might I consider providing a comment and if so, could I. . . .

I spin around twice, kicking up snow and laughing out loud, and run then through the drifts onto the road, heading home happy but more than just happy, amazed—and as thrilled as a gambler by patterns of chance and probability. What else in the world but *this* book, so propitiously titled, might have called me out early to walk in the fresh snow? Am I not, this winter's morning, a true student of weather? Nevertheless, far stronger than the book's coincidental pull, is a new friendship that seems, suddenly, enormously powerful.

On the lane to the house, I stop for breath at the olive grove and think how strange the green oval leaves appear, so thickly covered with snow. I pull a branch toward me and stick out my tongue, licking the lovely stuff off in one sweeping mouthful. The instant prickle of melting snow explodes in my mouth—flakes disintegrate like stars—as it transforms itself to a swallow of water. A sweet, chalky taste, and then gone in a gulp. Another mouthful and another, and I stand there for a long time, thinking of you and eating snow . . . far away in another country but, in my heart, home.

Elizabeth Hay is the author of *A Student of Weather*. She is also the author of *Crossing the Snowline* and *The Only Snow in Havana*.

LEARNING TO WAIT

JAMAL AND NAZIM are sitting on two cement blocks set against the barn, having a smoke and enjoying the late morning sun. I've brought out a tray of coffee and my homemade hazelnut biscotti. Nazim is crazy about these biscuits and says he wants the recipe for his wife: I explain that because it's an American recipe it will take me some time to translate and to figure out the measurement change from volume to weight. That's not a problem, he says, he can wait. And we all three have a good laugh, although not because he's made a homophonic wordplay—since we're not speaking English there's no pun available—but because Nazim and Jamal have always made *me* wait, that's what's funny. Ever since the summer of 1995 when I first came to this house and they began the work of renovation, they've been teaching me the fine art of patience. And I have been learning, with varying degrees of success.

The secret to easy waiting, of course, is *not* to wait, and to walk away from expectation with the same disregard as a bullfighter turning his back on the bull and trailing his cape in the dust. I know this, and yet that's simply not my nature: if I am expecting a letter, I am out to the mailbox at least nine times before the mailman delivers it; if I am waiting for email I am clicking Send-Receive like a gambler playing the slots. Still, after all these years, you will find me at the window mid-morning, leaning out and looking down the lane, frowning and cursing and busily demanding of the air, "But they *said* they'd come today. Where the hell *are* they?"

This, of course, is a question to which I know the answer. The chances are at least fifty-fifty that they're not coming: they just *said* they would because they knew that's what I wanted to hear. Like all workmen specializing in restoring old houses—a major business in this region where there's a good supply of tumbledown stone buildings and an increasing number of foreigners, like us, who are buying them—Jamal and Nazim are skilled not only in masonry, carpentry, electrical wiring and plumbing but also in straddling two or three jobs at a time. It can take weeks for them to finish even a simple bit of work: incorporated into any deal, either intentionally or unconsciously, is a kind of "maturing process" during which everything just sits and settles for a few weeks before a job is brought to its conclusion. Think of fruit in brandy. Like that.

In order to give the illusion that return is imminent, they generally leave their equipment and tools behind, *as if* they'll be returning first thing in the morning. The hammer lying carelessly in a corner is clear proof of intent—what better evidence of their word? Astonishing how much hope a cement mixer can generate if it's left in the middle of the driveway. After a week or two, however, cheerful anticipation is replaced by grim acceptance of the facts: these guys will turn up when they can and not a moment before. You have a choice—do the job yourself, or wait.

Jamal and Nazim and their fellow *ouvriers* in the building trade are quick to anticipate the moment when a client's frustration begins to edge toward rage, and have developed a number of successful ploys for maintaining everyone's equilibrium. Well before I can throw a temper tantrum because they've arrived several days late, they've cooled me down with one charming method or another. What most often sways me in their favour is Jamal's sheepish smile and open admission of guilt. When he ducks his head and mutters, *"C'est ma faute,"* I prepare to believe his explanation about why he was unable to phone last week to say he wasn't coming. There's another failproof routine favoured by Nazim, who adds a chummy shrug of complicity, the equivalent of "Look, I understand, I'd be mad too, but what can you do?" Accompanied by Jamal's solemn promise to get everything finished by the following Tuesday, this is usually enough to smooth things over. Until the next time.

Of the two, Jamal is the more believable because he's older and more experienced. He also appears to be a more polished actor, delivering his lines with such conviction it is easy to think that he means what he says. Over the years, however, we have noticed some repetition in explanations for why he and the others have not turned up on schedule. *Le camion est encore en panne*—the truck has broken down again—is so often the reason that I generally say it along with him as he speaks, or sometimes offer it up even before he begins. I now smile appreciatively when he brings out old favourites, such as "unexpected delay in shipment of materials," offered in the same way a schoolboy might try "the dog ate my homework." On many occasions, of course, he presents me with the truth: they're working on another site that is taking priority over ours. Sometimes, in fact, they are juggling so many different jobs that the only way to manage is to do a little here, a little there—and it all gets done, eventually. It just takes time.

Nothing happens overnight, they say. Look around. This is how things are, here in Languedoc, here in the Cévennes. This is not Paris, where life is hurried and stressful, this is the provincial countryside, this is the *south*. We have our own ways, our own pace. We are not slaves to the clock. That's why we live so long.

Both men are French of Algerian parentage; Jamal was born here, Nazim came as a child with his parents. Jamal is a fine-featured, handsome man probably close to fifty, with deep-set brown eyes shining with humour and intelligence: over the years, he has become our most trusted adviser on all matters concerning the house. Nazim, in his late thirties, is also good-looking but not as educated or refined in his manner as Jamal. Still, I've had a soft spot for Nazim since the morning we met during the first summer of renovation. He arrived ahead of the rest of the construction team to find me hacking my way through a sea of stinging nettles along the back of the house. It was evident I was not accomplished at wielding a scythe, and within seconds he had taken it from me and, with an amused grin, laid low those noxious weeds. An act of chivalry I force myself to remember on those days he does not turn up.

It is not a pretty house, Mas Blanc. It does not have a classic aspect or a stunning view, but like many a person of homely appearance, it has a good heart and an interesting character. Our part of the Mas is a plain three-storey stone building (the ground floor, now our cellar, once sheltered horses and goats, their slatted wooden mangers still on the walls) with a small stone barn beside it. There's a cedar hedge between our driveway and Bruno's yard but no proper lawn or garden, just a plot of land beside the barn where we have occasionally planted potatoes.

When I first saw the place, I was not certain that Bob's urgent desire to possess it was such a brilliant idea, but it seemed mean and counterproductive to turn against something he wanted so much. His several arguments in favour of France were reasonable and compelling, chief among them his decision to continue working after retirement as a communications consultant. Europe is that much closer to Africa and Asia where potential work would be, and from earlier years in Montpellier he had essential contacts. Besides, it was true that the cost of this property was minimal compared with buying a house in Toronto or Ottawa, those two cities where we would have considered resettling.

Although my own preference was to return to Canada, I had no feasible plan for achieving that desire. Besides, I was genuinely moved by Bob's passion for the Cévennes. His love of these hills might be rooted in his Huguenot ancestry or in the *auld alliance* between Scotland and France, but whatever its basis I did not doubt its strength and sincerity. I agreed to give his plan my best effort, remembering how much we had enjoyed a rural existence outside Belleville, Ontario.

This would simply be a return to those happy years—older, wiser, and in French.

Nevertheless, I couldn't see what had so charmed Bob that he believed Mas Blanc was the perfect spot. What I *could* see, as soon as I got out of the car and made my way up crumbling stone steps to a weather-beaten front door, was that this old house needed major repair, the kind of renovations we would not have the ability, energy or time to do ourselves. We were still living in the Philippines then, with three summers ahead of us to make the place habitable before Bob's retirement. As I wandered from room to room looking at all there was to do—the space meant to be a kitchen was bare except for a small and very stained porcelain sink—my spirits sank. I was ready to shed a tear of self-pity, perhaps even utter an oath or two. But I hadn't reckoned on the buoyant nature of William, the young English estate agent who had shown Bob the house and arranged the sale, and who was with us that day to hand over the keys.

A cheery soul decked out in gold jewellery, William is one of those Brits who always look on the bright side, who believe that after a nice cup of tea everything will fall into place. That plucky never-give-up spirit that saw England through the Blitz would see us through a little renovation, I was not to worry. He said he hoped we'd not mind, but he had taken the liberty of contacting a contractor he happened to know—reputable, cheap and available—who could come round the next day to discuss various possibilities. William had some background in architecture, as it happened, and he'd be pleased to help us out, he said, for a small fee, just ten per cent of whatever this contractor would charge.

The young couple from whom we bought our section of Mas Blanc had actually begun work a few years before but had found themselves to be badly suited both to fixing up an old house and to each other, and their divorce required them to sell the property. Some months after we signed the papers, we discovered to our slightly shocked amusement that the divorced woman was living with William. We now understood more fully his limitless enthusiasm for our hasty purchase.

And so, through William's intervention, into our lives came Roland, a round-faced, big-hearted Protestant from a nearby village, whose chief aim in life, we soon learned, is helping others less fortunate than himself, particularly refugees and foreigners new to the country. In those days, Roland's small company employed exclusively men who had trouble finding work for one reason or another, and that reason was usually their Algerian or Moroccan origins. Jamal and Nazim both worked for Roland then; today, however, Jamal and Roland are partners, with Jamal overseeing renovation and construction and Roland spending his time in good works. All the men we met in our years with Roland had North African names with the exception of Maurice, a toothless older fellow down on his luck, suffering from the ailment known as *"la maladie d'après-midi"*—after lunch too drunk to work.

Poor Maurice. The others treated him as their donkey, making him do the heaving and hauling, carrying buckets of debris down stairs and buckets of cement up. They said it was because he wasn't good for anything else, and at least this way he had a job. That was the summer they made a room for Abbey in the attic—breaking a hole for a window in the thick stone wall and inserting insulation under the tiles between the beams of the roof. It was horrible, hard work, especially in the heat. Who could blame Maurice for keeping a bottle in the barn for nips between trips to the attic?

But that indoor work came later in the history of Mas Blanc renovations. The first big job for which we hired Roland's team was the construction of a terrace on the north side of the house, shaded by the leafy branches of the *micocoulier* tree. Finding ways to stay cool is a major preoccupation in a place where the high cost of electricity makes you think twice about getting an air conditioner and where the heat in summer can be stifling. With William assisting as translator, we discussed with Roland the *devis*: proposed costs, materials and timing for transforming a window into a door and for building the terrace out of existing rubble and stone.

After everything was agreed upon, Roland assured us that the men would start work a week later, on Monday. That day we rose early, to be dressed and ready to greet them on arrival. We waited. We called Roland, who said, oh, he was sorry, there'd be a small delay, "because of materials." He couldn't say exactly when they'd come, but he assured us it would be soon. We waited for word the next day, and the next, and the one after that. Again, we called Roland, who said, oh, we never start a project on a Friday. Don't worry, they'll arrive next week.

Another week passed, and finally the following Monday we woke to the sound of water rushing out of an outdoor tap. "They're here!" we cried. "They've already begun to mix the cement!" We dressed quickly and rushed downstairs, expecting to see a gang of men up to their elbows in dirty work, building a wall of stone.

But no. There were three fellows in shorts and T-shirts, standing around having a smoke and chatting in an easy, good-natured way while they filled up a big plastic tub with water to keep their beer cold until lunch. They were a friendly bunch, shaking our hands warmly as they introduced themselves: chubby Abdul and his chubbier father, Momed, and Maurice with his lovely big gummy smile. They worked that day as they did most days to come, with the truck radio turned up full blast, until shortly after four o'clock, when they disappeared, as if by magic.

Now, I suppose we could have shopped around and found other workers. And I suppose we might have had our various projects completed more quickly, and possibly with more expertise. My old friend Charles, who lives across the Rhône in more fashionable Provence, says he never puts up with the kind of nonsense we do. If the workmen don't turn up, he voids the contract. If they don't deliver the goods, he finds someone who does, and if they don't do work well, they're not paid. Golly, I think, this sounds like very good advice. But then, if I'd done that at the beginning, I wouldn't know Roland or Jamal and Nazim, and I wouldn't have had so many laughs with Abdul. A man with the face and disposition of an unreliable cherub, Abdul no longer works for Roland; but for the first several summers he was here, and always jolly no matter what disaster befell. He seemed to be constantly wiping up spills or fixing things he'd broken—but all of it was funny to Abdul.

Other men than Abdul and his father might not have slanted the terrace floor toward the house, so that rainwater would lie in pools against the stone wall causing the interior wall to drip green with damp. But other men would not have so blithely re-tiled the terrace the following year—at no extra cost, Roland agreed—and given us yet another story to tell about the tricky process of turning a house into a home.

Most important, other men than Abdul would not have made me a garden at the foot of the staircase to the front terrace that he and Nazim were building during the summer of 1999. He made it for only one reason: he'd seen that I was in pain and he wanted to make me feel better. I had just been in a freakish head-on collision that demolished my car and broke my sternum: the day after the accident, I learned that my goddaughter, waiting for a heart-lung transplant, had died of kidney failure. Obviously, I could not fly to Canada to attend her funeral, and the sadness seemed almost too much to bear. When I transmitted this information to Abdul, I was standing at the front door in my pyjamas, tears streaming down my face, holding my chest and gasping, for speech was difficult because of the breastbone fracture. Abdul's eyes brimmed in sympathy, although he said nothing and just shook his head at such misery.

As the day progressed, however, he must have decided to do something to restore my joie de vivre. By the next afternoon he had made a small enclosure of old bricks to form a garden, in which he planted herbs and a few marigolds; when it was finished, he called me down from my bedroom to see it, asking if I would please now smile again. I was so touched that I declared the garden would be named in his honour. This struck

Nazim as the height of hilarity, and there was much laughter, just as Abdul had hoped. Of course, being the relaxed sort of workman he was, Abdul didn't really pay a lot of attention to method or materials, and Jamal had to rebuild the brick wall the following summer, cementing everything properly and making it right. But he agrees, with no complaint, that it is indeed "Abdul's garden."

He can afford to give credit to slaphappy Abdul, as he knows full well that we give *him* credit for nearly everything else. We speak of Jamal's kitchen and Jamal's bathroom and, indeed, Jamal's house: he knows, as we do, that Mas Blanc would not exist as it does without his labours, large and small. Recently, as he was finishing the electrical wiring for Bob's office in the barn, I asked if this amazing transformation—from empty space to a bright and attractive study—didn't make him feel especially proud. *"Mais, c'est normal,"* he said, with his usual shrug and smile, his tone giving the phrase several layers of meaning: yes, of course it's fine work. Why should that be remarkable? This is what I do for a living, it's not unusual as far as I'm concerned.

I laughed at that, and he did too, because *normal* is one of his favourite terms. Sometimes, as in this case, he uses it to indicate his dislike of too much praise and his distrust of the exceptional. But just as often he uses it to soothe my concerns, assuring me that what

I've perceived as a grave problem is, in fact, utterly commonplace. The door frame appears to be crooked? *C'est normal.* It's an old house, after all—right angles are an impossible dream. Don't worry. The roof is leaking after the rainstorm? *C'est normal,* nothing to fret about, just some tiles blown loose by the wind, easy to repair. Happens all the time, one gets used to it. Stone houses are endlessly forgiving.

Over time, I've come to understand that when Jamal says that a situation is normal, he means that there are flaws in the cloth and flies in the ointment, that one must anticipate problems and accept them as part of life. Whereas I've always thought that things are normal until they go wrong, Jamal's version of reality is causing me to readjust my expectations for fault-free existence and to regard the world in a more open fashion.

Normal may be one of Jamal's favourite adjectives, but more often he uses the adverbial form, *normalement,* meaning "ordinarily." This opens up a huge range of possibilities I have absorbed, slowly, as part of the waiting game. If I ask a direct question, such as, "Can you bring the gravel tomorrow?" his response will likely be an immediate, positive *"oui,"* but hedged with *"normalement."* Which means, barring unforeseen circumstance—acts of God, accident, death, or *le camion, encore en panne*—they'll be able to bring the gravel. It also means, quite clearly: but don't count on it. Because we both know that anything could happen between now and then.

Learn to wait, he is telling me, in his particular and gentle way. Learn to accept that life isn't perfect. *C'est normal.*

RAIN

WHENEVER I WAKE to the sound of rain—that insistent, relentless rhythm that gives a grey morning its own music—my first reaction coming out of sleep is always jubilation, a learned response from the years we lived outside Belleville, when a good pelting rain meant a cistern full to the brim. And that in turn meant, for a glorious, frivolous day or two, having as much water as we wanted for bathing, until we regained our senses and returned to the careful conservation of every drop.

In our old farmhouse on Marshall Road we depended on rainwater collected in the cistern for the washing of ourselves, our clothes and our dishes. (Our drinking water came from a well in the garden, a shallow and unreliable source that often dried up.) The cistern was a concrete cavern beneath the kitchen floor, accessible only through a small trap door set directly in front of the sink. When it was full, the reservoir held about four thousand litres, and we could open up the flap in the floor and reach down into the darkness and touch the cool surface or pick off bits of floating debris. In the fall there were always dead leaves and in the spring pale yellow flowers, courtesy of the tall old maples that shaded our house and filled the eavestroughs with seasonal offerings. In the winter we'd find foolish field mice floating from time to time: they would come indoors through the cellar and, no doubt mistaking the space for a haven from the cat, would fall into the water, drown, and bloat before sinking to the oozy bottom.

When it was raining hard, as it was yesterday, we could sit in the kitchen by the woodstove and listen to the cistern filling. The sweet, hollow sound varied, depending on the amount of water already present, and as the years passed our ears became so attuned that we could estimate volume without even looking. Had we been country folk in a book or a play, we might have leaned back in our rocking chairs and said, "Yep, she's jest about full up," or something of that ilk. But we weren't even *stage* country, we were city slickers who'd left Toronto to take up a semi-rural life.

In the years we lived in that farmhouse, we stayed amazingly upbeat about the problems posed by imperfect water supply. The well in the garden, dug decades earlier and lined with porous brick, allowed soil and, now and again, bits of strained earthworms through

the filter—an alarming addition to tea for the uniniti-
ated. As for the cistern, the water it provided was also
less than pure, although we chose to concentrate on its
virtues rather than its weak points. We spoke only of
rainwater's softness, the wonderful suds it made in the
tub, the sheen it gave our hair. We learned to ignore the
odours of rotting leaves, and we joked that the dead
mice gave our water body. We cleaned out the bottom
of the cistern during every summer's dry spell, for
there was always an accumulation of dark, stenchy
stuff to be disposed of. The dregs to a fine old wine,
we'd say, as Bob handed me up buckets through the
trap door and I carried them out to the compost,
holding my nose.

After eight years, we returned to normal urban life
when Bob took a job in Ottawa. We sold the house in
the country to sensible people who drilled a good deep
well, and we moved into a little frame house in a pretty
neighbourhood where instead of a garden beside us we
had a schoolyard, and instead of a well or a cistern we
had municipal water bills. Although we missed hearing
the happy rush and pour of water beneath the kitchen
floor, we admitted that daily life was easier in the city,
no question. You could turn on a tap any time of the
year and not worry. There was something to be said for
civilization and urban convenience.

But I could see that, when it rained, water simply
flowed off the roof and into the gutters and down

the spouts into the streets, rolling along the curb and into the drains of the city. Without meaning, without use, without touching us at all. After years of being on passionate terms with the weather, I was developing a remote relationship, no longer close and no longer involved. Increasingly, it struck me as sad and ironic that the only effect rain had was to cause me to carry an umbrella when nicking up the street to Len's Market to buy vegetables and fruits shipped from California where irrigation and spraying ensure that crops never fail. Of course, I knew how lucky we were. . . .

Picking up succulent produce from the bins, I would recall dry, hot Belleville Augusts when vines and stalks succumbed no matter how well they'd been mulched, and remember how heartbroken I would be to see my garden shrivelling before my eyes. Rain mattered then. Rain mattered more than anything. We would lie in bed at night and listen to the distant thud and roll of thunder and hope for rain. Clench our fists and *hope*. At the time, I believed we were suffering. Looking back, I see how deeply alive we were then, fused to nature and intimate with consequence.

It does not surprise me that we have chosen to live in the country again.

Two weeks ago we woke in the middle of the night to flashes of lightning and crashes of thunder, and the hard splashing of wind-driven rain against the bedroom windows. We were startled by the noise and surprised, because, although rain is par for the course, electrical storms don't normally occur in March in the Cévennes. When I couldn't count past one on my way to seven to figure the distance between light and sound and how close the lightning was, I knew we might be in for it, and sure enough, there was an almighty crack followed by the high whine of the computer's voltage regulator and the infernal beeping our refrigerator makes when the power goes off. Although it was a bit after the fact, we got up and stumbled around in the dark to unplug everything with electronic components.

Eventually we went back to sleep and, when we got up at eight, the thunder was still growling and snarling, and the rain falling thick and fast. Looking down from our bedroom window to the Ourne that ordinarily trickles along about fifty metres from the house, we saw not the tiny stream there'd been the day before but a mighty mud-brown river. Even through the closed window we could hear the water, a huge sound without fluctuation or rhythm, as if some beast were opening his throat and roaring without taking breath.

The Ourne cuts through flat vineyards in the commune of Latourne on its way down from the hills to join the Gardon d'Anduze, one of three tributaries named Gardon that become the Gard, the wide river over which the Romans built the Pont du Gard two thousand years ago. That astonishing aqueduct crosses the river near Remoulins, about sixty kilometres from here: designed to carry water from Uzès to Nîmes, what it does nowadays is bring tourist money pouring into the area. The little Ourne has a less illustrious history, but has served Latourne well for as long as there has been human habitation, which is reckoned back to prehistoric times.

Certainly the monks who made their home in the monastery, built on its banks at the tail end of the eighth century, would have drawn water for their gardens and for drinking. You can just imagine them, on a hot summer afternoon, running down to where a natural waterfall has made a deep pool known as the Gour de l'Oule, throwing off their heavy brown robes and diving in, perhaps praising God with a little plainsong as they swam. Nowadays, to the loud music of portable CD players, sleek young men dive there too, showing off for barely clad girlfriends who take their *bronzage* on the rocks. They build campfires and leave bottles and butts and all manner of garbage scattered about, noisy careless creatures who destroy the river's tranquility. Oh, what I wouldn't give for a naked contemplative or two.

We are fortunate, given these crowds, to have found our own swimming hole closer to home and inaccessible to anyone but us and our neighbour Bruno. Last year, while clearing brambles to make a path for hauling water to our new fruit trees, we came out on the bank to discover a deep stretch of clear water behind the dam. Because of the dense underbrush, we'd never had access to this section before, and our excitement was enormous—we were like kids for the next few days. We set stones into the muddy bank to make steps, and tied an aluminum ladder to a tree root for getting in and out of the water easily. Bruno made a towel rack of bamboo poles and branches, and brought a wooden pallet to serve as a changing-room floor. All of a sudden, we had our very own pool, complete with frogs and fish and dragonflies hovering over the surface.

By the middle of June we are in for a dip at least once a day, sometimes two or three if the weather is fine. Trees—linden and alder and birch and laurel—bend toward each other across the stream, their branches overhead forming a green canopy. Sunlight falls through the lattice of leaves in long strands, like shimmering green silk. Slipping into the cool water we almost always fall silent, as if we are entering a holy place devoted to worshipping the colour green. We swim up and down the green tunnel, in a secret world where everything is green— the shining leaves above, the dense underbrush below, the shadowy water, even the air. Green, we say, floating on our backs and watching the wind and light dapple the stream. We say green and we mean happy.

A whimsical local history suggests that the tiny Ourne is not only the heart and guts of Latourne, the Ourne is its mother. The author claims that Latourne is not so much the name of a village—that is, the houses and farms on either side of the Ourne—as the name of the terrain itself. He suggests that the word could be rooted in the ruined Roman tower *(la tour)* that became part of the hilltop château; or, possibly, springs from its proximity to the Gardon, which turns *(tourner)* as it passes under the cliffs in nearby Anduze; or indeed, might have originated with local potteries, for in regional patois, potters are known as *tournaïres* and there have been potters here as long as anyone can remember. *Pots d'Anduze* have been especially famous since their debut in the gardens of Versailles and for the last three hundred years local potteries have been turning out copies, shaped like old-fashioned eggcups. We have one, glazed deep blue instead of the more typical mustard yellow or muddy green: it sits on the terrace spilling out scarlet geraniums.

We rather hope it's the *tournaïre* connection that gives Latourne its name, for if that's the case, then Mas

Blanc plays a minor etymological role. A few months
ago a bearded, academic-looking fellow drove in our
lane and asked if he could walk about the property and
take some pictures. He explained that he was writing a
history for the Pottery Guild of Anduze and, according
to his research, there had been a pottery in the sixteenth
century where our house now stands. If his calculations
were correct, he said, we'd have a vaulted cavern in our
cellar where the original potter kept his wine. We took
him right down to the wine *cave* beneath the house
where he checked and measured the curved ceiling and
pronounced it suitably ancient and authentic. Now my
finding of so many shards of glazed brown and green
and yellow pottery in the soil of the garden makes
more sense, and as I come across each one I wash it off
and place it with the others in a large earthenware bowl
that sits by the front door.

Although we've seen the Ourne run high, neither
my husband nor I have seen it in flood, but we're
invigorated rather than worried or upset. I am
reminded of a typhoon in the Philippines fierce
enough to take roofs off houses in the compound
where we lived in Los Baños, for what I felt then was
not fear but excitement so deep that it was nearly
erotic: the thrill of watching palm trees, huge fronds

tossing in frenzy, bend to the ground—it was ecstasy, of a kind. The velocity of the wind and its deafening noise forced upon us acknowledgment of the planet's power to do as it chooses. Trees fell—one barely missed the house—our beautiful garden was in ruins, we had no water or electricity and, although I was concerned for Filipinos in circumstances not so safe and dry as mine, what I felt was not despair or terror but the clean sharp thrill of marvel. Even though I fully understood that typhoons are explainable—just warm and cold air currents meeting above the ocean—the event seemed so mysterious and awesome that I was full of wonder.

My emotions watching the river are similarly intense, and I urge Bob to get dressed so we can go outside to have a look. Carrying umbrellas and wearing wellies, we first go to inspect the fruit trees, fearing that the dam could cause an overflow into the field. However, it seems they are not in danger, for the river, although swollen, is flushing over the old stone *barrage* at great speed. We continue down the lane past our olive trees and on to the road to the Gour de l'Oule, above which is another dam. Along this part of the river—below the monastery and above—there are two old stone mills. One was ruined in the flood of '95 and the other, directly across from Mas Blanc, would seem from its decaying roof and empty interior to have been out of commission for a very long time.

Both mills had millponds, to which the waters of the Ourne are still diverted by small canals and sluice gates. The pond behind the mill across from Mas Blanc has a long chute, which descends under a wall into a conduit that crosses the stream in an aqueduct beneath a stone walkway, built in the seventeenth century. This pipe takes the water, by force of gravity, to a farm at least a kilometre away, where it emerges in a culvert and then empties into a narrow stone canal, edged with reeds and flowering plants, part of a garden irrigation system. Although clearly the system is full to overflowing this day, it seems as if everything is working as it always has.

We imagine there will be a spectacular cataract spilling into the pool at the Gour but the river is so high that there is no waterfall, only brown rushing water. The dam upstream is invisible as well. We decide not to walk farther—we feel too exposed and vulnerable as lightning begins again. We rush home and get a fire started in the fireplace, and when Bob goes down to the cellar and pulls the switch on the fuse box, the power's back on. Coffee. Life is good.

But the storm continues, the thunder rolls, the clouds hang heavy on the hills. There is no let-up—it just rains and rains and rains. "Well," we tell ourselves, "this *is* the Cévennes." We've read, and been told, that weather here has always been dramatic and unpredictable. Extreme conditions are nothing new, people have lived with drought and flood for centuries—in these hills every old farmhouse has a cistern as insurance for the dry season. Ours is not in the house, as it was in Belleville, but built into the ground below the retaining wall by the barn, where it takes in water that flows from a spring after heavy rain. We have never had to use it, although it was no doubt essential in previous periods of drought before water was piped out from the village. We look down from the terrace and see the spring rushing wildly into the cistern and out the other side to join the rising river.

When we venture forth again at noon, we discover our fruit trees shin-deep in water and sludge. We are much less cheery and sanguine. What if we lose those trees, after all the work it took to plant them in that stony field? The flood takes on a different colour, darker and more sinister, and we return to the house troubled, our mood utterly changed. But by early afternoon the storm moves back into the high hills, and the river begins reversing its madness. *(Okay, I was really out of line. I'm sorry, and I'll try to never drink so much again.)* The water, which had nearly covered Haddou's garden beside the house, recedes quickly, leaving us with a peculiar sense of loss. The big show is over.

Before nightfall we go out again to check the river, and witness the result of its temper tantrum. The dam near the orchard has held up, but the little stone stairway we made for our swimming spot has been swept away. So has the ladder. But no serious damage has been done, and the orchard, although a little the worse for wear, will survive. In the days that follow, we spend some time gathering up the leavings of the flood, and then— as does the Ourne—we go back to our normal rhythm.

As March comes to an end, so does our latest project, getting a workspace for Bob built in the barn. The beams are ready to be painted with antifungal preservative, and for that job we hire a local fellow whose name is Hervé. A handy jack-of-all-trades, he lives just the other side of the Cave Coopérative, not far from where the Ourne runs into the Gardon. He has a rosy face and a ready smile and exudes energetic good humour. He laughs as he tells me that of course he can work even though it is Easter. He's not bothered by religion, he says.

On Good Friday—not a holiday as the French take Monday instead—Hervé starts the painting at seven, and around ten takes a break and goes off for a stroll. Although not born in Latourne, he has lived here for nearly forty years and he knows the terrain very well, he tells us. He comes back after about half an hour, smiling broadly and offering us a basket of *morilles*.

One of the edible mushrooms Canada shares with France, the morel looks like a mad sponge that has decided to turn into a pointed hat. They're one of the sweetest rewards springtime can offer, no matter on which side of the Atlantic you find them: the poor man's truffle, rich and nutty-tasting when fried in butter with lemon and sage.

"How did you know where to look?" I ask, already savouring the treat in store.

"But of course I knew they'd be along the river," he says. "The Ourne is famous for them. Everyone knows that after a spring flood they'll be here by the dozens. Heavy rain in March is good for cleaning out the river, and it's even better for the land. *Everything* grows well afterwards. And look," he continues, "I've picked so much wild asparagus that there's enough for my family and for you too." At Easter, he tells me, it is traditional to make an omelette into which one stirs wild asparagus lightly sautéed in olive oil. Morels on the side, a little Merlot, some bread and cheese. . . . One can believe in the Resurrection with food like this.

We've just been learning, in the past year or two, to find wild asparagus as it comes up in March. It took a trail of older ladies coming along our lane with their plastic bags before we realized that whatever they were bending over to pick was possibly something we might like too. One of these ladies has a mean and greedy look about her, and I have tended to regard her as "the enemy" encroaching on my territory—although, because our lane is a public passage, she has as much right to the asparagus as I do. However, since encountering the generosity of Hervé, I have vowed to no longer give her my evil-eye stare and, instead, to smile warmly in a spirit of neighbourly sharing.

The asparagus-gatherers, for their part, no doubt regard *me* as the intruder: yet another *étrangère* coming into the commune that already has a non-French population increasing noticeably. In the past decade or two there has been an influx of Belgians and Germans and Dutch buying property in the hills, and although many use their houses only as holiday homes, they are a visible and slightly disconcerting foreign presence. I choose to think that those of us who settle here permanently—*définitivement*—are more kindly looked upon than those who just drop in for a few weeks of sunny weather. But I may be fooling myself. Just as I fool myself that this has been the worst flood we'll ever face.

LEARNING TO TALK

JAMAL AND NAZIM are sitting on their cement blocks out by the barn, having a smoke and enjoying the late afternoon sun. I've come out with two small bottles of 1664—*la bière blonde d'Alsace*—as is our custom at the end of the day. Offering a cold drink is something that Bob and I began as an occasional treat for the workmen during the first summer when renovations began, and over the several years that have followed, of continuing repair and reconstruction, the daily beer has become a firmly entrenched tradition. Since it is good weather we'll stay outside for this brief, pleasant ritual, but on rainy or cold days we might stand in the barn or come into the house to sit at the dining room table, where I'll join them with a cup of tea or, if it's late enough, a glass of wine.

This is the moment of review—of work accomplished or, if everything is going well, then perhaps looking forward to the next stage of a project. We might discuss the potential for problems that could slow things down—that damn truck again—or we might look through hardware catalogues for the best hinges for the cellar door. Most days, this takes between five and ten minutes, no more. But at the end of the week, or after a particularly difficult job has been completed, there's a more relaxed mood and conversation wanders, another beer is offered (they *are* small) and talk turns to other matters. This is my French Lesson, the lab in which I practise, expanding my vocab and improving my pronunciation. This is where I am, finally, learning to talk.

Unsurprisingly, Bob's better than I am at male chat, and he is also less inhibited and intimidated by speaking French. Still, in my own slow way I find my confidence growing with Jamal and the others, for they do not laugh at my Anglo accent and they seem to enjoy helping me learn and pronounce new words. And, it must be said, I do my homework. In order to participate in these conversations, I follow sports more than I have ever done before so that, if necessary, I can start things off with the French equivalent of sowhadjathinkuvdagamelasnite? (*Vous avez regardé le match?*)

Watching football or rugby is no hardship. Reading the local newspaper, *Le Midi Libre,* is more work, but essential for keeping up with what's happening in the region, as well as staying on top of current events—a daily *ragoût* of political scandals, strikes, highway blockages and *manifestations* of wine growers or farmers or students or doctors, a mention of which inevitably opens the way for discussion of high-level corruption, racism, unemployment and the European Union. There's always something to talk about, unsurprisingly—because talking is an essential component of life in France. As teenagers in *lycée,* the French are trained to think and speak logically, to analyze arguments and reason out sound rebuttals. As adults, they seem to like nothing better than heated discourse, particularly around a dinner table that provides several others with whom to engage in emotional, and not always rational, debate. This is an oral society: people love to talk and they love to eat, and they love to do both together.

We see the workmen talking as they're having lunch, out by the barn or on the bench overlooking the old mill across the stream, as they most often choose to eat on the job rather than go to a café. Especially during our first two summers of renovation when there were many men on site, lunchtime meant a sudden end to labour and a convivial assembly around a red metal folding table set up in the shade at noon sharp. Stools, or cement blocks serving as stools, would be placed around it while the men washed under the hose and then retrieved baguettes and lunchboxes from their trucks and cars.

Out of these boxes came not only food—thermoses of soup, containers of salad, meat and vegetables, jars of yogourt and fruit, rounds of cheese—but also plates, cutlery and glasses. It wouldn't have surprised me to see linen napkins appear. Generally water or beer was used to chase down the first part of the meal, but a bottle of red wine would always appear for the cheese course. During these leisurely lunches there'd be much animated exchange and lots of laughter, followed by short naps on the grass or in a truck. *Déjeuner* sets itself apart from labour and becomes a time devoted to food and talk and relaxation—companionship in its truest sense, the breaking of bread together, giving the workday its proper centre and meaning. (We began to understand this as we sat on the terrace in silence staring at our pitiful little tuna fish sandwiches.)

It's not only our workmen who take long lunches: in the south of France lunchtime is the *heure sacrée*, the holy hour that's more like two. Everything closes— banks, business offices, stores; shopping malls and *hypermarchés* may stay open, but they are the exception. In this context, the large commercial enterprises seem to be a North American addition to the French way of life, aggressive consumerism at the expense of healthy family-centred tradition. At noon in the towns and cities, there is a wild flurry of traffic as everyone who

can, goes home, and streets are jammed with impatient
drivers honking their horns. If you can't get home,
you go to a restaurant or you carry with you the ma-
kings for a proper meal. Good food and wine make
you feel happy. What can be the purpose of life if you
are not happy?

It was during our second summer of renovation that I
met a perfectly happy man. It was one of those days
when Mas Blanc was buzzing with activity: two men
retiling the roof (it had been tiled a few years earlier, just
as William, the real estate agent, had said, but so badly
that there were leaks everywhere), two men with chain-
saws trimming branches on the huge *micocoulier* tree and
three men pounding with drills and hammers up in the
attic, making a small bedroom under the eaves. The noise
of people and machines was deafening, and to this was
added, late in the morning, the sound of the enormous
ramonage vacuum being used to clean the chimney.

The *ramoneur*, an attractive fellow in his fifties with
bright blue eyes and red cheeks, whistled and sang as
he worked, old folk tunes mixed with popular standards. Heard above the background din, his singing
seemed particularly sweet. When the time came to
write his cheque, joking that I should also be paying for
the concert, I invited him to sit down and served a

small black coffee. Perhaps these are polite country ways everywhere, but I have learned here that one does not simply pay for work done, one engages in a social transaction, which usually involves some drink appropriate to the time of day.

We were joined at the table by my daughter, whose abilities in French far exceed my own; as this rapidly became apparent to the chimney sweep, he asked how she had become so fluently bilingual. Abbey explained that she had been educated until the age of ten in the Ottawa French immersion program and then attended *collège* and *lycée* during the three years we lived in Montpellier in the early 1990s. The city is only an hour south of us, yet it seems like a different world— Mediterranean climate and architecture, sophisticated, cosmopolitan and, yes, frenetic by comparison with the slower pace of life in the hills.

Eager for conversation with this nice man, I asked if he liked Montpellier. He smiled broadly and replied that he wouldn't know since he'd never been there. At first, we thought he hadn't understood my question, and then we thought he was jesting, but he assured us that no, he was completely serious. Why would I go to Montpellier, he asked, his tone of voice making it clear it was a rhetorical question. I am happy here. I love the Cévennes. It is where I live, and where I work. I am Cévenol. I do not need to go anywhere else. This is where I belong.

Well, I said to Abbey after he'd left, when you go off to university in the autumn you'll probably take some first-year philosophy course in which you'll be asked to examine the classic question: What is a happy man? Now that you've actually met one—they're terribly rare, this is the first that I've ever seen—you can write an A+ essay. You've aced the course.

The following year I called him to have the chimney cleaned again—our insurance policy demands an annual *ramonage* certificate—but was told by his wife that he'd had to leave this line of work because his lungs were bad. The man she recommended in his place arrived next day and set to work without singing. Instead, he talked. Large and jolly, with thick ringlets of dark hair and a gold ring in one ear, he talked all the time he was cleaning and for an hour after as we sat with our coffee. And all my quick generalizations about "insular Cévenol attitudes" went up the chimney like smoke.

This man, Jules, told me he works very hard for ten months and for the other two travels. Now that his children are old enough, they come along with him and his wife to his favourite place in the world: Mexico. Over several years he taught himself Spanish so that he could get around Mexico more easily, and now they head right up into the mountains, where they live in a remote village with native people whose language he has also learned. Jules already knows more about Mexican history and culture than I'll *ever* know about his country, and is filled with a desire to know more, a desire that even he doesn't understand completely. But he knows that although he's content in his work and life in the Cévennes, his real happiness resides in that mountain village across the ocean.

I tell Jules how well I understand him, for I too have a place I love to go. My longing is not for the strange and exotic so much as for the familiar, for the agreeable sensation of belonging. Indeed, I seem always to be looking for a duplication of emotions experienced "back home." But I explain that, unlike him, I did not have to learn another language in order to fall in love with Tasmania. I did nothing. It happened like a thunderbolt to the heart.

Some wag or another has put it about that spending time in Tasmania is like revisiting the 1950s and for this reason I'm occasionally asked, by those who know me to have a nostalgic turn of mind, whether that's what drew me to this small island at the bottom of the world. Get out a map and look—there it is, floating off the lower, eastern end of Australia, as ignored and mocked by mainlanders as Newfoundland has often been in Canada, and in the same way made the butt of stupid jokes. I begin to explain to Jules how unfair and unwarranted this is.

But he stops me and says he wants to know how my attachment began. His interest in Mexico blossomed years before he set foot in that country, nurtured by reading and research. For him, going to that place represented the realization of a dream. This sounds to me very logical and planned, establishing and then achieving a goal—highly admirable, in fact—and I feel, by comparison, careless and random in my attitude to life, for I admit that I landed in Tasmania ignorant and innocent, having had no burning interest beforehand. It was only upon inhaling the air on my first visit that I became addicted.

I tell Jules how it happened. In early 1995, while living in the Philippines—before I'd set eyes on Mas Blanc—I was invited to participate in the Salamanca Writers' Festival in Hobart. On arrival at the airport shortly after lunch, I was met by one of the organizers, a writer of children's books who had his infant son with him, sleeping in the back of the car. He explained that a convention of mainland dentists had booked all the hotel rooms, and I would thus be billeted with a family, but no one would be home until four. We had three hours to spend, and what to do? Did I like to walk?

We drove halfway up the side of Mount Wellington, the moody blue mountain that looms over Hobart, to a parking lot where I changed my shoes and he got the baby into a backpack carrier. Within half an hour of the plane touching the tarmac, I found myself hiking up a steep mountainside path that wound through the mottled, peeling trunks of eucalyptus trees. All my senses were functioning at an extraordinarily high level of intake: the rich, gummy perfume of the trees, the sound of them creaking in the wind, the long view down to the shining Derwent River and the city lying peacefully along its banks. And beyond that, rolling hills and then nothing, I realized, nothing but frigid blue water between us and the ice of Antarctica. I felt the ecstasy that comes when everything dovetails. Each aspect of the world around me—colour, shape, smell, sound, texture—seemed perfect, exactly right in a profound way. It occurs to me now that my excitement was partly due to being out of the humid green heat of the Philippines and in a climate where my body felt more at ease. But all I knew then was bliss, and I guessed, correctly, that the impression being made upon my brain would be indelible.

At four we arrived at the handsome Victorian house where I'd be lodging. My host, a cheerful fellow who'd just come in from work, explained that he had to join his wife and children at their school fête and urged me to make myself at home; they'd be back in about an hour. He showed me my room, gave me instructions on where to find the tea and the kettle and asked if there was there anything else I needed. As I had to attend a festival occasion that evening, I asked if I could use their iron to get my outfit ready. "No worries!" he said, and showed me the ironing board already set up in a corner of the dining room. Then he left and I was on my own.

And *that's* the moment, I tell Jules. Me, humming and happy, the smell of gum trees still in my head, ironing in the dining room, cup of tea on the sideboard. I expected the strong feelings I'd had on the mountain to fade, but as I ironed, it seemed as if those first hours were being pressed into my soul. The house was still, the way houses are at the end of the afternoon, resting before the bustle of suppertime. Everything in the room, just as on the mountain, seemed utterly familiar, as if I'd papered the walls myself and hung the pictures. I could live here, I thought. *I know where I am.* And when the family came through the door at five, I was startled by their intrusion, so completely had I made the place mine.

When I finish my story Jules' expression is quizzical, for my explanation does not seem to translate properly to his ears: her *passion* began while she was *ironing?* Can I have understood her correctly? But we just leave it at that, and accept that we both know the pull to be elsewhere.

There is much more I want to tell him, but I decide to save it for his chimney cleaning next year, when we may talk about the differences between Mexico and France, and he may ask what the weather is like in Tasmania. I'll talk then about how often there are rainbows, sometimes many in a day, and how the sky seems to have a unique luminosity day and night, even in cloud or pouring rain. It may be a result of something as dire as the hole in the ozone layer, but whatever the reason, I feel when I am there as if I too am shining, as if light is filtering through my pores. Although there is much that is dark and sad about the island, both in its history and its landscape, in Hobart I feel as if I am light itself. I want to tell Jules: When I am in Tasmania, I feel wings growing out of my back—but fear he will think I am mad. Metaphor seldom survives translation.

Years later, on a fourth visit to Hobart, I am sitting in the Rétro Café on Salamanca Place, drinking coffee and talking with Christiane, an elegant, dark-haired Frenchwoman with whom I have been acquainted since 1995. As always, we begin by speaking French and, as always, we turn to English as soon as the conversation takes on complexity and depth, for not only is she fluent in my language, she teaches it. She asks rather wistfully if I am feeling settled in France yet, and whether it is starting to feel like home.

Oh yes, I say, the process is definitely underway: I make a point of sounding positive when anyone asks, believing that the more true it sounds, the more true it will become. The renovations are nearly complete and the house is quite comfortable, I say, taking out some photos from my bag to show her. We have all our books on shelves now, all our favourite things placed in such a way they seem to belong, and all our pictures hung. We've built two terraces, one for catching the sun in winter and another that provides a cool, shady spot in summer—that one overlooks our neighbour's garden and, at the foot of our property by the stream, a large stand of golden bamboo and a hammock hung between two young oak trees. We've planted twelve fruit trees near the olive grove and we'll have our own apples this year. Paradise, I say.

But what about friendship, Christiane asks. What about people? I admit that we lead a quiet and rather isolated life, but we do have friends and acquaintances, some of them new and some dating from years spent in Montpellier. We have joined a walking group composed of English and French speakers, most of them retired and all of them enthusiastic hikers who love exploring the Cévennes. There are other friends as well, with whom we go to concerts or the cinema in Nîmes, or with whom we have long, chatty Sunday lunches. When we go into Anduze for groceries, we are recognized as "regulars" not tourists—I am on a first-name basis with Isabelle in the fruit and vegetable shop and with Jean-Claude at Le Petit Jardin, and not a week goes by that I don't have a chat with Yvonne the postmistress.

But to tell the truth, I say, I do find it hard speaking French and I am often lonely. In some ways, I may be more *chez moi* in Hobart than in Latourne. "Here's the evidence," I say. "I never get lost. I always know where I am. Maybe it's because there are landmarks, like Mount Wellington and the harbour and the river, but whatever the reason, I feel totally confident whether I'm driving or walking. I never need a map, I seem to know instinctively where to go. I've never made a mistake yet."

She shakes her head in disbelief and laughs. She has lived here with her Australian husband for more than thirty years, has driven her children around Hobart to countless lessons, sports events and birthday parties, and still gets lost. "I never know which street goes where," she says. "Sometimes I just have to pull off the road to collect myself and get my bearings. I don't know where I am."

Her dream, she says, is to go back to France in her old age. Her children will scatter the way children do when they become adults, and besides, with jobs so scarce in Tasmania these days, young people do not stay, they head off for Melbourne or Sydney or parts unknown. Without the pull of family, she imagines she will be free to return to where she belongs. Her greatest fear is that she will die and be buried here. She wants to think of herself, although her *self* will no longer exist, being interred in French soil. She is obsessed by this need to leave Tasmania before she dies, to know that her bones will not come to rest in this place. "Is that so strange?" she asks, her bright smile embarrassed, vulnerable.

I smile back and confess that in the early morning when I cannot sleep, I too fret, not about death itself but about the disposal of my remains. I am surprised at such dark thoughts and imagine that by acknowledging them I can diminish their weight and gravity. I tell her I am grateful for the intuitive rapport we share. Never mind whether our dialogue takes place in English or in French, we speak each other's language of the heart, and we have acknowledged a secret dread only those who feel cut off from their homelands can share.

Months later, back in France, I am sitting in my study, reading over these notes and pondering how food and death can braid themselves together and how talking about one thing leads, strangely, to another. As I am unwinding my thoughts, I hear the doorbell and run down to find that Bob has opened the door to Jamal, dressed not in workclothes but in a light wool pullover and slacks, with his wife, Anne, a small, pretty woman with short auburn hair and a vivacious demeanour. Anne and I have not met before, and I am embarrassed to be caught in baggy old writing clothes when she looks so trim and stylish, in that way that Frenchwomen seem to manage effortlessly. Jamal explains that he has always wanted to show his wife where he has spent so much time over the past six years, and they happened to be in the area. He hopes we are not busy, they only intend to say hello.

We are immensely pleased and insist they come in to have a "proper visit." As I get coffee ready and put out a plate of cake—and the biscotti that Anne says Jamal has mentioned; she wonders if she could get the recipe—Bob takes them on a tour of several exterior renovations for which Jamal has been responsible. The star in her husband's crown, Anne is told, is the broken-down stone wall he reconstructed last year, twenty metres long and nearly two metres high, an enormous task gracefully rendered, for the stones are placed in such a way that there seems to be a melodic line to the curve of the wall. At its base, he constructed a concrete tunnel for a small spring that runs through our land down into an eighteenth-century cistern set deep in the ground with only its red-brick roof showing. Now, as various flowering herbs I've planted take root between the stones, the wall has ingratiated itself into the garden landscape, although its real function is not decorative but protective; it is a retaining wall for the property alongside the stone barn where, thanks to Jamal, there is now an office upstairs.

I ask Anne, as they come back into the house, if she sees how essential her husband has been to our life here. She nods and says she already knew that, for over the years Jamal has described his projects in some detail, the problems and difficulties as well as successes such as our superb kitchen and bathroom. She indicates, with a smile, that she's heard some of the stories woven into our Mas Blanc mythology. For example, she says, she knows about the crisis of Abdul's wrongly slanted terrace, and as we go upstairs she reminds me of the day the entire stairway caved in. I am amused to think that she knows the same stories we tell about fixing up this house, and wonder how much a different point of view changes the details, and the narrative tone.

The four of us spend an hour chatting and sharing anecdotes about old-house renovation and all that it entails: the expense, the labour, the stress for all concerned. Eventually, I bring out photo albums so that Anne can look at "before and after" shots to fully appreciate the progress that's been made since we first contracted Roland and his team. The albums are kept in a handy spot in the living room, as they are needed nearly as often as the French-English dictionary sitting on the shelf above. If we are reminiscing about a particular job with the workmen during the end-of-day beer, photos are brought out as proof of accomplishment—especially if a new worker needs to be impressed with miracles already wrought. And sometimes we look at them on our own, as if to reassure ourselves that we have been part of these changes.

When Jamal and Anne leave, they invite us to their house for a couscous dinner in a few weeks' time. We accept and respond with assurances that the long-promised barbecue for everyone who has worked here will take place this summer. "It'll be perfect," I say, "now that everything's going to be finished by the end of May. Isn't that right, Jamal?"

With his usual shrug, he replies, *"Oui, bien sûr. Normalement,"* and Anne laughs along with us, for she is evidently familiar with the phrase.

As we wave, watching them drive off, I feel my stance shifting slightly. I can no longer claim that I am isolated and lonely because I can't speak French—I've been conversing for over an hour with people who appear to understand what I say and, not only that, who clearly want to be friends. It seems a bit ironic, now that I think of it: had Bob and I already spoken the same language as the workmen, we might not have tried so hard to communicate and would simply have gone about the business of getting everything done as quickly as possible, without hours spent talking and talking and talking. Instead, here we are. On the fine, lovely edge of something new. Something other than *normal*.

HOMAGE TO KENKO

From the window of the Writer's Cottage, above Salamanca Esplanade near the harbour in Hobart, I can see a full and lovely rainbow making an arc over Mount Wellington this early October morning. One side is double and the other end has dipped into grey cloud and disappeared, as if it were slowly dissolving. Spring weather in Tasmania is famously giddy, and at this very moment there is rain on one side of the cottage and sun on the other, black thunderclouds along the hills to the south of the city and to the north, clear blue skies streaked with white.

I look again and the rainbow has gone. Although I know it is simply because the angle of sunlight on vapour has changed, I feel responsible for the loss because I let my attention wander. One must never waver in one's beliefs—in rainbows, in love, in goodness—or else, you know what happens.

I have returned to Hobart as writer-in-residence, and am given this renovated nineteenth-century cottage in which to live and work for a month. Settled at last in the Cévennes, I have come back in part to see whether my declarations of love for Tasmania have any substance or might be, like the rainbow, simply sunlight and vapour, a dream.

My first visit here seemed—in fanciful terms—predestined, the result of a delicate chain of coincidences. Asked to recommend an author for the annual literary festival in Hobart, the wife of the Canadian high commissioner in Canberra offered my name, having met me once in Ottawa and knowing I was then in the Philippines, for at that time we both wrote regularly in the "Letters Home" column of the *Ottawa Citizen*. Government-subsidized airfare for a writer would be, obviously, less expensive from Manila than from anywhere in Canada: I was an ideal choice.

And so, if it hadn't been for Bob taking the job in Los Baños, and if, and if. . . . I enjoy tracing the filigree of linked events that took me to Australia. But do they matter, these fateful conjunctions? It is movement forward one ought to focus on: the future, not past. However, imbued since childhood with the notion that we *should* be aware of history, and that museums hold the most accessible convergence of things we ought to know, I go to the Hobart Art Gallery and Museum, looking for visible clues to explain my attachment or, at least, to understand the island more completely. But the paintings and the artifacts seem to illuminate all that is brutish, short-sighted and tragic in human nature, and although I believe that nothing that happened here is worse than it has been anywhere else, my own country included, I leave the building wishing for a beach without footsteps, devoid of story. I attempt to restore my spirits by walking down to the harbour and watching the movement of boats and birds. I buy a bag of fried scallops on the pier, and life takes on a more genial aspect as I fling bits of food to the red-eyed gulls who whoosh down with greedy joy.

It has become my habit in Hobart to give creative writing workshops in the schools—besides providing a little extra income during my stay, it has been the means of meeting people with whom I have much in common; over time, many have become true friends. Strangely, as the number in Canada is depleted—through death, or unresolved quarrels, or from the fraying of old ties—more are appearing here. These new, warm friendships seem like compensation, as if there is a certain quota the universe has dictated.

Friends' School has invited me back for another visit and I am glad, for I like this old Quaker institution, its awkward cluster of buildings sprawled over a hill-side. When I am here, I fantasize an alternative reality: teaching senior English, directing the annual play, maybe running a little poetry club after school on Thursdays. But in reality I have come for only one day, to lead some writing classes and to speak to the weekly school assembly, which happens also to be a prize-giving day. Friends, as it is known, rewards individual scholarship and creativity, but—so it seems—never at the cost of communal integrity, for they have found the right balance between the one and the many.

Over lunch in the staff room I chat with a teacher who has just returned from a sabbatical art tour through Russia with a group of other women. Along the roads out in the countryside, she tells me, lines of impover-ished peasant women held up glass jars of sweet wild strawberries for sale. And when the bus stopped so that the women on the tour could buy one or two jars, they were rushed by scores of ragged women crying out in Russian, "Buy mine, buy mine!" The teacher recalls how frightened and upset she was, because selection of one meant rejection of others, because she was face to face with the visible repercussion of choice. And—unsaid—because all players in this vital game of chance were women, that made it worse.

I am reminded of the road we often travelled from Nairobi to Nakuru when we lived in Kenya, where, if we stopped at a stall for rhubarb or potatoes, we would be mobbed by young boys trying to sell rabbits or plums. We got used to it, over time, and had a variety of ploys to keep as many boys happy as possible and to get away as fast as we could, but it was never easy, and we were always silent in the car afterwards.

Now, because of a chance meeting in a Quaker school in Tasmania, my brain reels out superimposed images, double exposures depicting that moment of having to choose: squat Russian peasant women wearing kerchiefs tied beneath their chins, shouting loudly and thrusting up jars of red berries, overlaid with bright-eyed black-skinned boys running along the dusty ochre shoulders of a highway, holding out live rabbits by their ears.

One of my closest friends in Hobart is an English teacher named Liz with whom I have great rapport— we read the same books and we laugh at the same things as if we've known each other all our lives. Yesterday, we drove out of town and walked around Opossum Bay for hours, mostly through meadows gone mad with yellow flowers. They seemed at first glance a type of black-eyed Susan, but they are named Capeweed, Liz tells me, originating in South Africa. Like so many other plants and animals brought into Australia from abroad, their presence has proven invasive and disastrous. Pretty it may be, but Capeweed is a pest: poisonous for grazing animals and an irritant to human skin. At the end of the hike my trousers and boots are covered in bright yellow blotches of pollen, evidence that I've been walking through fields of gold. The kind of detail one could use, Liz and I agree, as a clue in a murder mystery or in a tale of marital deception.

As we walk, she tells me stories about her Tasmanian family. On her mother's side she is descended from a girl named Maryann sent out at fourteen from Ireland for stealing five chickens to feed her hungry brothers and sisters. Later, when she was given her pardon, Maryann married a soldier met when she was working as a convict maid in Hobart, and with him founded a large family. Her eldest daughter, also Maryann, was determined her children would receive a good education, and the family produced several scholars through the years. Liz was born in Launceston, at the top of the island, where her mother was a schoolteacher and her father a barrister-solicitor who loved the wilderness. He leased from the state an island on a small lake in the highlands, accessible only by an eight-hour climb through heavy bush. He designed and built his own foldable canvas-and-plywood canoe he could carry on his shoulders, and with this, plus his pack and tent, he'd go in for weeks at a time, always with another bushwalker for safety, but never with his children, for the island was simply too remote.

When Liz was nineteen, he finally took her along with one of his usual walking companions, another lawyer. The men, accustomed to being on their own without a girl listening, spoke Latin when they didn't want her to catch on: suddenly, it was not a dead language but a secret one. Now, nearly forty years later, Liz is retiring and tells me she is planning to study Latin for her own enjoyment. She has inherited her father's passion for walking as well as his island, and someday, the next time I come, she'll take me there.

Two weeks ago in a laundromat café, as I was nursing a latte and reading Hobart's daily, *The Mercury,* a couple about my age sat down nearby. We struck up a conversation after the man asked me to pass the pepper from my table, and I thought he wanted my paper. We began by laughing about the confusion caused by our different accents, and within minutes were exchanging names and phone numbers. The woman, Penny, said that every morning she drives out to a beach about half an hour from the city to breathe the fresh sea air. She invited me to join her and said she'd call: Hobart being as friendly as it is, I knew she would.

Today Penny and I drive down to South Arm, discovering common friends as we quickly sketch our lives. After parking the car at her old farmhouse, she leads me through boobyalla scrub to the shoreline facing Storm Bay, where the wind rushes against our faces so vigorously that it feels as if we are being scrubbed by the air. The wide beach is deserted, for the sea rolls in too violently for swimmers, and only the most adventurous surfers ever dare its towering waves. We walk in silence, looking out at the horizon for whales. They do not appear, but I don't mind. I am perfectly content. This is exactly the empty beach I was hoping for when I left the museum.

Later, I tell Penny that I am writing about Tasmania—or, more precisely, about my own uneasy ambivalence. I profess to feel at home here, and yet I back away from engagement with the island's history. I joke that perhaps what seemed like true love in the beginning has been only a flirtation, a variety of geographic promiscuity. Even though I learn the names of trees and flowers and birds and animals, and use many rolls of film recording occasions with friends and encounters with the natural world on my travels around the island—giant ferns, baby wallabies, beautiful waterfalls, snow-capped mountains—I remain at an emotional distance, as if I know in my heart I can never stay.

It seems imperative, if one is going to write deeply about a place, to acknowledge the past and to illuminate the many ways it attaches itself to the present. Several historians and novelists—some island-born and others from away—have dealt with this brilliantly, and I read their works with awe and admiration for the authenticity and passion with which they have brought to life characters both real and imagined. I am feeling discouraged, I tell Penny, since it seems that everything I've written since arrival has turned out to be confused, without any discernible pattern. Instead of writing stories, I am only making notes.

Penny suggests that if I can find ways to connect with the indigenous people who were here long before the French and the Dutch and the English, then the true spirit of the land will energize and focus my writing. Fine, I say, but how? Those Aborigines who were exterminated by white settlers did not leave behind visible evidence that might give me some sense of their presence. To get started, I always need tangible things, I tell her—like stones.

She smiles, and tells me to wait. We have already left the long beach, and now we walk down around a large lagoon where black swans float dreamily in circles and other water birds—oyster catchers and hooded plovers—wade in the shallows, prancing around in a comic way, as if they are on stilts and doing a little dance to raise some laughs. The lagoon is ringed by stringybark gums and coastal peppermints under which we stroll, talking, when suddenly Penny puts her hand on my arm, and we stop.

Ahead of me I see two grey stones, side by side on the ground. One is about the size of the double-volume

Oxford dictionary, with a long, shallow indentation across it, clearly made by human intent. Beside it lies a round stone about the size of a man's fist. What I am looking at, Penny tells me, is a grinding stone, unmoved since it was left in this place by departing members of the Oyster Bay tribe, who roamed freely on this land until the 1830s when they were rounded up—ostensibly for their own good but, tragically, to their utter and complete annihilation.

Until this moment, the gentle slopes around the lagoon had seemed devoid of human presence, with no evidence of habitation or cultivation now or ever. But here before us is this small sign of daily life led at its most elemental level, two stones I would have missed seeing without Penny's direction. It occurs to me that they represent exactly the wordless point at which I intersect with Tasmania. Simply existing in the moment is enough.

Near the Parliament buildings in Hobart is a long wall into which old gravestones have been set, stones that tell something of the sad but glorious story of brave settlers who died so far from home. Deaths from drowning, more from fever and childbirth, more still of infants and young children, few from ripe old age. Many are familiar Tassie names—Pit, Mason, Cook, Pegg, Underwood—but others are archaic English

ones like Tidd and Snook and the marvellous moniker
Scattergood Kemp.

But I like these clean and ordered stones far less
than those discovered in small forgotten graveyards
overgrown by weeds and grass, often weathered so
badly that inscriptions and names now are random
indentations to be deciphered slowly, if at all. Up in
the village cemetery of Wynyard on the north coast, I
found wonderful names, like Joseph Thunder, and two
brothers, Ett and Urk. Closer to Hobart, on a point of
land near Price Bay, in a grove of pine trees shading a
dozen sandstone markers, I read on each stone the
same birthplace—Coll, a tiny island off the west coast
of Scotland. I've been to Coll and remember it as flat
and bitterly cold except for the beery warmth of the
hotel pub. How thrilling it would have been for these
Scots to find themselves in this verdant place after hard
months at sea, and to believe they had escaped their
harsh and dreary homeland. But not only their place of
birth is the same on all the stones, their date of death
repeats itself as well: 1857. No sooner arrived and
ready to thrive than they succumbed to cholera.

Even the success stories of those who did manage to
survive are fraught with loss and disaster, resem-
bling classic Canadian settler-tales of hardship and

disappointment before difficulties are overcome. What interests me most are the women at the centre of the action, the brave and resourceful wives who, like Susanna Moodie in the Ontario bush during the same period, managed to keep moving forward through calamity and misfortune.

In a family history called *Kettle on the Hob*, I follow the life of Anna Maria Cotton, matriarch of the Cotton family. In 1829 she sailed from England with her husband and their children to take up residence in a thatched sod hut prepared by Dr. George Story, a close family friend and a Quaker like themselves. After Anna Maria had unpacked their trunks and set all their possessions in order, she began her preparations for an evening meal that would mark the first day in their humble home. Helpful as always, George directed one of his servants to hand down a side of bacon hanging from the roof. Holding a candle to help the fellow find it in the dark, George set fire to the thatch: the flames spread so rapidly that the family escaped with only the clothes they were wearing. Everything brought from England burned to ashes. Everything.

I think of this story as I drive past the Cotton family seat at Kelvedon, a handsome white house set among pastures edged with hawthorn hedgerows, the very picture of English prosperity. Anna Maria lived to a ripe old age and saw her family flourish, saw with her own eyes how wise she had been to follow her husband to this far-off land. But did she, I wonder, ever forgive George?

At the end of my stay, I spend a week alone in the beach house belonging to a Canadian and English couple, both of them writers. Although we've never met, through mutual friends they have invited me to use the place in their absence. I rent a car and drive up the east coast through rolling, sheep-studded landscape until, by arrangement, in Swansea I meet people who give me the key. Half an hour later I have installed myself, amazed at such good fortune. The house, set on a rise overlooking a huge bay, has walls of glass, creating the sensation that even indoors you are part of the sky and the sea and they are part of you. It is as different from Mas Blanc—built of stone to protect you *from* the world rather than allowing it entry—as a dwelling could possibly be.

The first evening, sitting on the cedar deck with a glass of Tasmanian Pinot Noir, I orient myself as the sun sets. The village of Swansea twinkles down the coast to my right, and to my left the pink granite mountains of Freycinet National Park lie across the wide inlet of wind-whipped water. It delights me that I have come here entirely by chance, *par hasard* as the French would say, for these mountains are the Hazards.

A flurry of clouds drifts over the distant peaks. Some of them get pulled down into shadowy clefts in the rock, strands of silk caught by a stitch into rose-coloured velvet, but most cruise along like good-time girls fluffing their furry wraps, passing by on their way to the dance hall. I watch the sky until it darkens and the stars come out, so many and so large they must jostle for position.

The next day, I drive to Freycinet and go walking, climbing up and then down to reach the brilliantly clear turquoise waters of Wineglass Bay and then a steep hike back again. The speckled, freckled nature of landscape in Australia is nowhere more evident than here. The peeling trunks of eucalyptus trees are mottled olive-grey and pewter and burgundy. Out in the open, boulders are peppered with black and orange lichen but, on the sheltered forest path down to the bay, they are patched by bright green moss and silvery lichen. Where the hills are bare of foliage, long black streaks scribble down the striated rock-face of feldspar and quartz. All around me is sun and shadow, stipple and stripe. As I walk, I try to recall in its entirety Gerard Manley Hopkins' poem that begins "Glory be to God for dappled things"—and amuse myself by imagining how a visit to Tasmania might have changed his imagery.

I have come to this house by the sea to write, but instead am spending my days in silent contemplation of cloud and sky, or in gathering shells and stones along the white sand beach where I never meet another soul. At night, I climb early into bed with books gleaned from shelves around the house, wondering if some word or idea will appear to galvanize the flow of my thoughts, to help put order into my gathered notes and jottings. On the fifth night, I pick up a small book, *Essays in Idleness (The Tsurezuregusa of Kenko)* and realize that I have found the organizing system I need.

None at all. I will do as Kenko did.

A Buddhist priest, Kenko was also known by his lay-name, Urabe no Kaneyoshi. Between 1330 and 1332, during a time of much political turmoil in Japan, he wrote down his thoughts, 243 fragments of varying length, which he pasted to the wall of his cottage (although this story is in dispute, I favour the idea of wallpapering a room with words). His Buddhism shapes and underlies his views of the world—the impermanence of all things, the endless cycle of birth, growth and death, and the vanity of human achievements and possessions.

This work belongs to the random mode of composition called *follow the brush,* a form congenial to Japanese writers and readers who felt that it was "less dishonest" than creating fiction. In other words, it did

not impose pattern on experience and it did not transform reality: instead, the relaxed reader encounters
apparent formlessness and, in moving from one subject
to another, enjoys tracing subtle links between them.
The work of making patterns is left to the open-
minded reader—allowing an infinite number of varia-
tions to occur.

I read the book quickly, and then I begin again.
"The most precious thing in life is its uncertainty,"
writes Kenko. "In everything, no matter what it may
be, uniformity is undesirable. Leaving something
incomplete makes it interesting, and gives one the feeling there is room for growth."

Later that same night, awake because of the noise of
wind and rain slapping against the glass, I turn on the
light and look around the bedroom for something else
to read. I pick up *Promises, Promises,* a book of essays
on literature and psychoanalysis by Adam Phillips,
assuming it will put me to sleep. Instead, I read through
the storm.

In a chapter on clutter, I read how a teenage boy
dresses each morning by throwing his clothes in a pile
behind him and then picking what he's going to wear
with his eyes closed. Clutter, says Phillips, invites us to
make meaning in the absence of pattern. Clutter tanta-
lizes us, lures us into a relationship with material in a
way that is far more seductive than discernible order. I
read on, delighted to have so inadvertently discovered

exactly what I want to believe. "In clutter, you may not be able to find what you are looking for, but you may find something else instead. Clutter may not be about the way we hide things from ourselves but about the way we make ourselves look for things. It is, as it were, a self-imposed hide-and-seek."

It feels as if coming to *this* house, and picking *these* books to read, has had in its chancy juxtaposition something of divine revelation. I've always had a penchant for doing this, opening books at random, letting words or phrases leap out to show me the way—for decades, I have turned to *The Books of Knowledge*, my grandmother's encyclopedia, and riffled through the pages looking for answers whenever I am in doubt. Here in this glass house, without knowing what I was looking for, I have found *reason* in the disorder of my reflections, and not only that: justification.

There is no other way for me to write about Tasmania, because I am still wondering, still putting the pieces together. I may spend the rest of my life working it out, and that'll be just fine. I quote myself some lines from Rilke, understanding them for the first time: "Be patient toward all that is unsolved in your heart. Try to love the questions themselves. Do not seek the answers that cannot be given, because you would not be able to live them. And the point is, to live everything. Live the questions now."

MAKING UP MOTHER

MY MOTHER IS THE SMALL, slim woman in the centre
of the black-and-white photograph I have lost. I cannot find it anywhere, but I can see her still, standing in
her bare feet on the divide between dry beach and wet
sand. She is dressed exactly like the two women who
stand with her, in a black jersey bathing suit over which
a pair of men's white trousers is loosely belted. There
are three men in the photograph too, wearing the same
outfit, black tank-top bathing suits and baggy pleated
trousers. All six have their arms linked and their hands
in their pockets and they face the camera in a jaunty
way, as if to say. . . . What? What are they saying? I try
to imagine, but I can't hear, I don't know.

But I'm pretty sure where they are: Port Stanley on
Lake Erie, less than an hour's drive from London,
Ontario, where my mother and her friends are nurses

and the men medical students or interns. Although they are dressed identically on this private excursion, back in London at Victoria Hospital the young women will be capped with bonnets of starched white cotton and clothed from neck to shin in it too, and the men will have shirts and ties beneath their long white coats over which they will wear, like a badge of office, the stethoscopes marking them as superior beings.

My mother has bobbed hair, and it appears to hang straight down as if it is wet, which indicates she has been in the water. In those days she must have been as *sportive* as she looks in the picture: her shoulders are firm, her arm muscles nicely defined and her waist indented smoothly above the belted pants. She has an athletic-looking body, nothing in appearance like the rounded and bosomy mother I recall from my girlhood. She put on weight easily then because she got so little exercise, inactive not from laziness or lethargy but from fear. Fear of pain, fear of dying.

Because the mitral valve of her heart was damaged by rheumatic fever when she was twenty-two, she spent the rest of her life unable to run or swim. In later years she could not even climb stairs without shortness of breath, and her lips would turn blue at the slightest overexertion. Oh, she'd still put on her bathing suit and get in the water with Ruthie and me, and on summer holidays we'd sit and splash each other in the shallows at Bruce Beach on Lake Huron, but she could no longer do the crawl or the breaststroke. If indeed she went swimming this day—she never minded cold water, she would have plunged right in, laughing—we can date the photograph, for it would have been taken before the end of May 1933. It was then that she fell ill.

Ruthie and I have slightly different versions of our mother's medical history, but that is not surprising as, given the five years between us, we deviate in many remembrances; we come to the shared events of our lives from our own perspectives, as siblings do. We have, in the past, occasionally suffered over our disagreements, but slowly, with age, I am learning a great truth about recollection; there *is* no truth, and inconsistencies only add to the richness of mutual memory. Between us we include several, if not all, of the possibilities.

What we recall in common is that our mother knew she was sick that spring, perhaps even knew that she had rheumatic fever: her body ached, and she'd taken her temperature and found it to be extremely high. But instead of reporting this, or seeing a staff doctor, she took aspirins every few hours to keep going so that she could graduate with her class when the day came. What this meant, years later, was that she frequently spoke of her guilt—she herself was responsible for her invalid condition. She herself had betrayed her body. From this cause and effect, my sister and I were meant to take an essential lesson, which was that this personal tragedy had been "brought on herself." The point was, obviously, that downfall, heroic or not, is always a result of *hubris*—thinking you know better than you do.

It was an important year, 1933, the fiftieth anniversary of Victoria Hospital's nursing school. There were meant to be fifty girls graduating that year, and our mother, Catherine Innis MacLennan, couldn't be absent or the magic number for the Golden Jubilee ceremony would be spoiled. Traditions and special occasions were always important to her, even at that age, and she felt sure that her attendance mattered. Wonderful, to believe so purely in the necessity of one's being in the right place at the right time. Wonderful, but wrong.

It is here that Ruthie and I diverge, veering off into two different stories or, at least, different endings. Here is hers (more likely the correct one, although I still tell mine).

Graduation day arrived, and Catherine managed to get to the ceremony without any of her supervisors discovering that she was sick, although many of her friends knew and in various ways had helped hide her condition over the past several days. Her mother, Belle MacLeod MacLennan, had come down from the family farm near Ripley the day before, and was in the audience to see her daughter walk across the stage to receive her diploma. A young intern—no doubt someone who had been part of the group keeping the illness secret—sitting near our grandmother was heard to say, "That girl ought to be in bed." Indeed, as she walked off the stage she collapsed behind the curtains and was taken immediately to the hospital, where she remained in bed for many weeks. Nevertheless, she had the satisfaction of knowing she had not let her classmates down.

My version is that the night before the ceremony there was a dinner and dance for the graduating nurses and their escorts. Catherine was looking particularly beautiful, with sparkling eyes and high colour in her cheeks. During the evening, as she was dancing with an intern, the gravity of her condition made itself apparent as he felt the heat from her face and her hand in his. "My God, you're burning up, Catherine," he said, and took her back to the residence immediately and sent her to bed, at the same time notifying the superintendent of nurses that he believed my mother was seriously ill. Within an hour she was taken to the hospital, and had to endure next day the terrible disappointment of not being part of the ceremony.

In the photograph, as I remember it, there is nothing to indicate which rendering of her history might be the true one, my sister's or mine. I catch no glimmer of triumph or failure, I see only my lovely mother standing there in a line of six, smiling into the lens. And now, too many years have passed and there is no one to ask.

The sauciness of her expression and the devil-may-care posture could signify either story, the brave young woman who makes it across the stage, or the one who is swept off the dance floor and out into the June night by the virtuous young doctor-to-be. Was he, perhaps, this dashing young man beside her in the sand? Or maybe it was the moustachioed fellow on her other arm, soon to be the husband of her friend Alicea, who stands with both feet in the lake, long hair tangled around her face and her body voluptuous in the black jersey swimming suit.

The six in the line are the material out of which a story can be made, but I could not look into this photograph, even if I were to find it, and discover how the tale turns out. There would be no shadows on the skin to indicate the way the lives will go, towards the light or into the dark. There is only my mother's pretty, smiling face, and her haunting voice from my childhood, heavy with sadness: "Oh, if only. . . ."

My mother, wanting to tell me who she was, and so many times telling me—but I heard her with the ears of a child, inattentive and self-absorbed. And now I must make up the stories without her.

What interests both Ruthie and me, and catches our imagination, is the man she stands beside, who may be, we speculate, "the man she didn't marry." We both remember being told about a hard-drinking medical type she feared would turn out badly and so, although she loved him, and loved the light, quick way he danced, she ended the relationship. Neither of us can remember his name now. Jack? Eddie? However, the point of the story was clear and embedded itself in our young brains: "Don't be fooled by romance, girls, only settle for a man of good moral character."

But she was crazy about him, we agree on that. We got the impression that she knew what it was to have your heart beat so fast you can't breathe—not because blood isn't pumping properly through your arterial valves but because desire is so intense that your blood has become heavy and viscous, laden with lust. She never said that, of course: we gathered it by the way her face would flush when she talked about the beau she had rejected. Which is why, I suppose, I like to imagine it was he who said, "Catherine, you are burning up." Murmured low, with a kind of smile, leaning into her body and brushing her face with his hand as he looked down into her feverish eyes.

Maybe they were lovers. My sister and I consider this question, and she says, oh no, definitely not. She remembers our mother telling us not to give way or we'd be sorry, remembers her telling us that sex is only beautiful *after* marriage. Still, I find myself speculating, suspecting. If this guy in the photo *is* Jack, or Eddie, he definitely looks like a fast mover, the way he's standing there, cool and sure of our mother's affection. Cocky, that's what.

He looks a little like a rooster, now that I remember the photograph more clearly, the way his hair stands up like a comb on his head. Do you think he wanted it like that, or was it a cowlick he couldn't manage? Women love men with uncontrollable hair, they're always wanting to slick it down with their hands and then ruffle it up again. Did our mother lie with him in the sand that day and run her fingers through that hair?

Who was he? We could find out, we could look him up in the medical school yearbook, we could do some research and set the facts straight. Why don't we ever go further with our game of making up?

Oh, we say, maybe this fellow in the photo is not the one. Probably it just happened that on this weekend he was part of the crowd going to the beach. But really, we are too smart for this lazy ruse, my sister and I: we know how, when you are digging down into the past, everything means something, everything is a clue.

Eddie, Jack—how did he bear it, when she gave him up? She told us she could see that he was going to be a drunk and even in the black-and-white photograph I remember a visible flush, high on the cheekbones and over the nose. That fine thin Scottish skin—or Irish, one of those fair Irish redheads—but for sure the love of the booze is there. She saved herself from a life of despair by knowing how to read the signs, by looking forward and imagining the worst. How careful she was on the one hand, how careless on the other.

And so Ruthie and I sail through the years carrying the invisible photograph between us, telling our stories back and forth, clinging to our fabricated versions of history, making up mother as it suits us as we move through our own lives. My stories are essentially tragic, full of regret, and hers are more upbeat, allowing our mother that moment of glory as she strode across the stage before her world came tumbling down.

I have the pearl buttons from her nurse's uniform, and my sister has the navy blue wool cloak with the red lining. These are holy relics, for our mother made of her nursing years something out of which she instructed us about life—her value system, her sense of female identity and personal integrity inextricably tied to her vocation. Because of her heart condition she was not allowed back on the wards where the work would have been too much for her; she had planned to be a pediatric nurse, but caring for small children all day long was now out of the question. More disappointing, she was told she ought not to have children herself, when and if she got married.

So she became a private duty nurse and during the Depression worked through the registry the hospital supplied for individuals in London who needed home care. She lived with three other nurses in a little apartment not far from Victoria Park, and in her travels around the city she saw the squalid conditions of the poor and the mansions of the wealthy. The work she did gave her a far richer understanding of human nature than she might have had in a hospital ward, an understanding that came down to us in her stories, long anecdotes involving people from all walks of life, and that always moved to a moral finale in which good was rewarded and evil met with some dreadful end. She had a string of stories about her nursing friends too, some of them tales of loss or disappointment, offered as proof of what happened if one allowed sex to addle the brain. She taught us what she knew from living through the "Dirty Thirties" but whenever she used that term she always looked a little embarrassed as if dirty meant naughty. She must have had a life, then, no matter how frail her heart.

Sometime after the start of the Second World War, she began playing bridge with a group of nurses in an apartment on the top floor of a house owned by a young married couple who often had their own bridge parties and social evenings. Often she and the others upstairs could hear someone playing the piano below, current hits and popular standards being chorded with a rolling left hand, the sound of someone playing by ear. By now Jack or Eddie had long departed, and the stage was set for her to meet the pianist, our father, and marry him.

I do have a framed photograph of my mother, which sits in a niche by my bedside. Something very peculiar has been happening to it in the past ten years or so, and I study the picture daily to see if this process continues—and it does. Indeed, it seems to be speeding up in a way that alarms and troubles me. Day by day, my mother is getting younger.

When I received it from my father, shortly after her death at age sixty-three, the photograph showed my mother as she was in May 1970, at age fifty-nine, on her one and only trip to California. My father took the shot just after they arrived in their hotel room in San Francisco, a city she had long wanted to visit, ever since her Aunt Margaret (her mother's adventurous sister), had worked there in the '20s and '30s, and had come back up to the family farm on the sixth concession with tales of glamour and romance. My mother has a corsage of small, faded pink roses pinned to the lapel of her raspberry-coloured wool suit, and she is smiling in a stiff, unnatural way, as she often did in later years. Her thick dark hair is cut short, and there is no visible grey, although I am certain she never dyed it. Her brow is slightly furrowed, through the embarrassment of posing for the picture, but her face is unlined, her features fine and even, her blue eyes deep-set and intelligent. An attractive older woman, who had weathered by that point several operations including two rounds of heart surgery, first to clean the mitral valve and then to replace it with a plastic one. She took various drugs after that, including a blood thinner to keep the valve from clogging, and which may have been responsible for the hemorrhagic stroke she suffered in the winter of 1972, which led to her death from another stroke two years later.

I had been married a little over a year and was living in Toronto when my mother had that first stroke. My father phoned the high school where I was teaching to tell me what had happened, and I went directly to the principal with the news that I would be taking a day's leave and would miss a parent-teachers' night scheduled for that evening. He attempted to bully me into staying for the event. "Your mother's not going to die immediately just because she had a stroke," the principal said. "Why, people often linger for *years* afterwards." A stupid, thoughtless man.

I drove that evening to Kitchener where she lay in the hospital, unable to move or speak normally. In the days that followed she regained the power to move her limbs, but her speech was garbled and when she tried to write down what it was she wished to say, her wavery script was indecipherable. Although she had been in hospital many times before, this was different. And she knew it. She understood what had happened, and that made it worse. She had cared for stroke victims during her home-nursing days and, farmgirl that she was, had always said, "If I ever have a stroke, take me out to the back forty and shoot me." And now here she was, and no one was going to do that. She was trapped.

Slowly, over the months that followed, she became "nearly herself" again, but there would always be a slight hesitancy in the way she moved and spoke, as if she were not entirely certain that she had said or done something correctly. Her facial expression was often that of a bewildered child who had awakened in the middle of a bad dream, and frequently her face crumpled in frustration. I visited on weekends, and realized as time passed that our relationship was reversing itself: At twenty-nine I had become the mother, and she, at sixty-one, the child. In the summer of that year I drove her up to see her sister Norma in Ripley, and then on to Lake Huron, in hopes that seeing familiar places and people would bring back memories, and indeed it did—but she could not express herself, language kept failing her. Near Kincardine, we sat beneath a tree, holding hands, looking out at the lake and sky, two women by the water's edge, watching the horizon as if for some sign. "I'm not right," she said, as tears slid down her cheeks.

However, she was to make astounding progress in the time she had left. A few years before, the American actress Patricia Neal had had a massive stroke, and her husband, the writer Roald Dahl, organized a rehabilitation program for her with the help of a therapist and the entire English village in which they lived. For several months, following a rigid schedule, a roster of volunteers kept the actress working at fever pitch to recover speech, to relearn language, numbers, concepts, until eventually she was able to return to acting. The success of the scheme was documented in a book, and with this as his guide my father began a similar effort for my mother. Day after day, loyal friends in Elmira came to the house, an hour or two at a time, to prevent Catherine from sinking into depression and to help her do the carefully organized homework laid out for her.

Dad was gentle but firm during this long process, never losing patience as he kept her attention focused on recovery. Every morning, he would write out a page of questions for her to answer before lunch, when he would give her a new set for the afternoon. To begin with the questions were simple—what colour is the sky?—but as the weeks marched on, they became increasingly difficult, drawing upon her memory and knowledge. She'd always loved to play bridge, but after the stroke she couldn't tell a heart from a spade. So the cards would be spread before her, and with help she'd repeat their names until she could go through the deck unaided. By the following year, she could enjoy a game of bridge again, write out a grocery list, carry on a conversation, prepare meals and lead something like a normal life: but she was increasingly sad, and often spoke of her wish to die so that my father could marry again.

None of my mother's heartache shows in the photo. Only this astounding rejuvenation I see happening, day after day. The older I get—I am her age now—the

younger she becomes. She is more youthful in appearance than many of my friends. She looks like the kind
of woman I'd want to know better, someone with
whom I might feel comfortable enough to ask intimate
questions, and to share my own thoughts and feelings.
We could go out—a glass of wine in a café, say—or
stay at home with a pot of tea, and really get to know
each other. We would have a grand time, and she
would tell me everything.

Sometimes I feel as if I *am* my mother when I stand out
in the early evening, watering the flowers and lilac
bushes we've planted along the broken-down stone
wall behind the barn at Mas Blanc. How odd this is, all
these years after her death, having her so clearly in
mind that I feel as if I have become her. Holding the
hose at this particular angle, I feel I am repeating in my
pose her very being, as if I am duplicating in some way
the essence of my mother's *self*. And what is that? Who
was she?

I call Ruthie in England to see if we can work out the
meaning of this simple act. Does this moment illuminate our mother as a passive invalid in statue-like
repose, or as nurse and nourisher making the garden
grow? We talk, we find images, but no easy explanation for why this might be important. Our mother

exists in our memory in her patterned cotton house-dress, standing on the front lawn, and we see behind her the white house in which we spent our childhood—but we are unable to define her or know her heart.

We know that she is making sure the peonies that came from our father's mother's garden get a good soaking, for they had to be kept in excellent condition or else my grandmother had fits when she visited. That's a whole different story, we agree; the tension between those two women who loved the same man (albeit it from different points of view) is not part of what we are trying to discover here. And so we go back to the memory of our mother standing peacefully on the grass with the hose in hand, waiting for neighbours to come over to chat when their own watering was done.

We begin remembering the neighbours, both of us relieved of emotional weight by this diversion, but realizing too that we are on to something, for her relationship with other women—friends, family, neighbours—was central to our mother's life. To know her we must see her as she was with her friends, talking. She loved to talk. As we consider how much we resemble her—our women friends so essential to our well-being, both of us capable of running up enormous phone bills—we begin to remember who she was more clearly. We see her standing in the twilight with other women, heads together, voices soft, sometimes a laugh or a sigh. We recall there was one we both liked because she was young and pretty, not at all dowdy as seemed to be the normal fashion for married women in those days. She wore Avon perfume and eyeshadow and lipstick, and her long auburn hair was always just so: she'd mince across her lawn and over to ours, the only person we'd ever seen, outside of movie stars, who wore high-heeled shoes with shorts. As we look back from this vantage point, we realize that, to put it bluntly, she was a real *babe*.

It was her husband—slightly older than she and rather reserved in his manner—who cautioned our mother when I turned fifteen that she should "do something" about me and that I not be allowed to go out barefoot around the neighbourhood or downtown on my bicycle, as was my custom. The implication (my mother had some difficulty imparting this to me) was that bare feet were sexual objects and, as such, not socially acceptable.

I was fascinated—utterly enchanted, in fact—by the notion that feet were sexy. It had never occurred to me, for I had certainly not conceived of my long-toed size elevenses having anything to do with love. (I was so young, that's what I thought sex meant: I didn't understand a thing.) It was true that I did like to go barefoot from spring until fall, and the soles of my feet grew so tough that, having already begun smoking in secret, it was my private delight that I could strike a match on my bare heel to light a cigarette. I remembered that fastidious neighbour a few years ago when photographs were published of an English duchess having her toes sucked by a lover on the edge of a swimming pool. Aha, I thought. So that's what was in his middle-aged mind. Did my mother know that?

Yet again, my sister and I have sidestepped the difficulty of remembering our mother and drifted off into other stories and recollections. We start the process and then we move away, as if there is something we cannot or do not want to find. We know she loved us—she gave birth to us in spite of medical advice—and we believe she loved our father. We know she was brave and kind: but was she happy? And why do we even suspect that she was not? Somehow our memories are clouded by the dark years before she died, and we cannot see clearly back to who she was before.

And so it goes. From time to time, we walk the beach of remembrance, trying to make something of what we find. Sometimes memory casts up treasures for us to retrieve and ponder, but we never dive deep in search of more, as if we fear the current, the undertow. We make up mother from dreams and scraps, working backward out of what we want to know about ourselves, about the choices we've made, and why.

I begin listing other ways in which I feel I duplicate her movements or her stance. Changing pillowcases is the first thing that comes to mind, and pulling the sheet into a nice tight hospital corner. Such a simple thing, making the bed—and with the smell of fresh white cotton I inhale my mother's presence, and the connection between us causes a spark in my brain, a lightning moment of love.

But she is gone. There is no way to retrieve her, there is no longer anyone who can tell us who she was in the way we want to know. Once, a number of years ago, I went to visit her best friend, whose name was Dot, and asked her to tell me about my mother. I wanted details, anecdotes, secrets they might have shared, truths hidden from children. "She was a wonderful woman," Dot said, her elderly voice tremulous and her eyes lit by private remembrance. "Just a wonderful woman." That was all.

FAST WATER, SLOW LOVE

WHEN BALLOU DIED at age sixteen near the end of the millennium, I gave him the best funeral any cat has ever had, going so far as to break out the duty-free Talisker being saved for some special occasion. As far as I could see, this was a special occasion, and beloved Ballou deserved to be seen off with a proper wake. Perhaps because I was alone, Bob on a consultancy in Uganda and Abbey looking for work in Toronto, I felt the responsibility more keenly—as well as some relief that there was no one around, not even Ballou, to see me standing out by the mound of his grave that dismal November afternoon, glass of whisky in one hand and hymnal in the other, singing all five verses of "Abide with Me" and choking with sobs on the really good lines: "Swift to its close ebbs out our little day."

Ballou's health had been in decline for several months, the slow wasting of kidney and liver disease, so that his death was not a shock but the sad end to a long wait. Two veterinarians in the Anduze clinic had provided differing points of view on what could be done regarding his unavoidable demise. One, a gruff man of great practicality, said we should just bring the cat in and he'd put him down. The other, a younger fellow with very nice eyes and a finer sensibility, declared that unless the animal was in pain there was no point in killing him sooner than he would die naturally. When asked how we might discern if Ballou was suffering, in order to make a decision, he said that unless the cat refused to be touched or hid himself away, we could rest easy.

Much preferring the second course, we let Ballou take his own sweet time, watching him slowly grow thin and his fur lose its sheen and turn raggedy—but having him with us, alive. He never seemed to be uncomfortable; he simply spent more of his life snoozing, in various patches of sunlight—moving from room to room as the hours demanded—or on the old rocking chair by the fire, or on my lap. Because he went outdoors much less, his claws did not wear down and as a result he could be heard around the house, the ticky-ticking of his toenails on the tiles a sound both delicate and sober.

When he took his last breath he was resting on the duvet plumped up at the end of the double bed, a location he had claimed as his own over the years. His grey body seemed, in death, very light and small—just as he had been when he came into our family in 1984, given me by a farmer outside Ottawa who was getting rid of a barn cat's litter. Although this one was the sickly and runny-eyed runt, I was immediately smitten and took him home for Abbey, who had just turned seven and wanted a pet. Little did we suspect what a hardy little creature he would turn out to be, adapting to each new setting as we took him on our travels from country to country. He became "the heart of the home," no matter where we were—a solace to each of us in the way he would make himself available when wordless companionship was necessary. Finally, at Mas Blanc, he was able to relax: we assured him there'd be no more nasty trips in the cage he so hated, and no more butter on his paws for the first weeks of adjustment to a new house. He could enjoy old age, taking walks with us down into the tall grass by the Ourne or sunning himself on the warm terrace. This was it.

And now, this was it. I laid him down on a white shawl of Ethiopian cotton with a border of purple and silver, a finely woven piece of fabric befitting a fine cat. I wrapped him carefully leaving his head bare, and then placed him on a folded scarf in a wooden wine box I'd obtained for this purpose from an organic vineyard just over the hill from our house. Big enough for six bottles of wine, it was too large for Ballou's body, but

I had much else to put inside besides the cat. In the manner of the ancients, I added to his makeshift coffin various objects to see him into the dark: a candle, his collar, his bell and a small can of duck liver paté; a photo of the family as we were in 1984 and another of our front garden in Ottawa; a shell from the Philippines, a pebble from the Cévennes, a sprinkle of soil from Kenya and a red rose from Bruno's late-blooming bush next door.

I placed another scarf over him and patted him goodbye before hammering down the wooden lid. I wrote his name and the date on the box and carried it outside, noticing how light it seemed in my arms.

I had already dug a deep hole—kindly as always, Bruno had helped with no mocking smiles at my eccentricity—at the corner of the stone wall surrounding the land behind the barn, where our clothesline is situated with a view of the ruined old mill and the stream below. As we don't have a clothes dryer, and as European front-loading machines are small, washing is done frequently and taken out to the line every day or two. Ballou's resting place would be visited on a regular basis, which seemed appropriate: he had been with us for such a long time—how could he not be now?

A few weeks later I took the next step, ordering a stone engraved with his name, to be set flat on the ground and surrounded by flowers. In the yard of the monument company, I chose a small piece of polished grey granite, fully expecting to be treated with disdain by the stone merchant, a rugged-looking fellow who didn't seem the sentimental type. To my surprise, he spoke in a soft and sympathetic tone, asking if the name indicated a dog or a cat. And how old was he, *madame?* Ah, then you must be very sad. Yes, we understand. We receive many requests similar to yours.

Weeks later, as I go out to the line to bring in dry towels and look down at his little stone, it occurs to me that Ballou's solemn burial rites have been my replacement for all the real funerals I have not attended since I left Canada. So many friends and relatives have died— more than a score—and their passing has been mourned from abroad without benefit of comforting social rituals. I phone my sister in England to discuss this notion, for I know she will understand my position—it is hers, too. Did we ever imagine, I ask, that we would grow up to feel bad about *missing funerals?* How pathetic, we say—and our tone is ironic, searching as always for the comic line to pull ourselves through.

With the passage of time, I've become accustomed to not looking down from the upstairs window at the outhouse in Bruno's yard. In fact, I don't really think about it much anymore. But since my return from Canada in September, I am training my eyes on the other side of the house as well, learning to peer out across vineyards to St-Baudile but not downward to the trees and gardens below. For there *are* no trees or gardens now.

Where Haddou's artichokes, tomatoes, beans and potatoes grew only days ago in long, straight rows, there is only rubble and sand. Where our stand of bamboo swayed in the breeze there is bare rock, and where we hung our hammock between two slender oaks is only water. Where the new stone wall—so beautifully built by Jamal to look as if it had been there forever—curved protectively along our property, is now a depleted and muddy bank out of which the long brown roots of the *micocoulier* dangle and the exposed pipes of the septic system hang out with nowhere to go. Debris of all kinds—chunks of cement, torn clothing, shredded plastic, bits of metal—lies scattered across an expanse of broken stone that, when I left for Canada in July, was green with grass and wildflowers. Most pitiful-looking of all is the ancient cistern at the base of the wall, which has had its red-brick roof sheared off, leaving the reservoir open to the sky and filled with sludge.

Nothing is the same since a gargantuan flood in early September swept everything away, everything but the grey-white limestone that has emerged, misshapen and barren. That rock has the cruel look of giant bones—clavicle and hip joint, scapula and pelvis fused together in some terrible accident—but it also seems bleached, as if it has been long exposed to the harsh sun. In fact, until the raging river washed the soil away, this *calcaire* had not seen the light of day for centuries. Not since records were first kept in 1610, say historians quoted in the *Midi Libre* newspaper, has there been a flood of this magnitude in the region.[†]

We know how blessed we are that Mas Blanc is standing high enough above the Ourne that the house itself has remained essentially unharmed—between here and the Rhône valley, several people drowned or were injured, and thousands more watched their homes and cars and livelihoods disappear in the space of a few hours. It is a disaster of enormous proportions, seemingly incalculable even though helicopters whap overhead daily so that politicians can look down

---

[†] The rain and resultant flooding in the *département du Gard* in the south of France on September 8-9, 2002, were the heaviest and worst that have ever been recorded here. In one day, the area received the same amount of rain that Paris ordinarily receives in a year. Of the Gard's 353 municipalities, 311 were inundated and 295 of them declared disaster areas. In all, 85 percent of the *département* was under water, and 97 percent of its population affected by the flood. Hundreds of kilometres of roads were washed out and many vital bridges collapsed as rivers rose as much as seven metres in a few hours. More than 100,000 telephone lines were cut, and power and water supplies were unavailable for several days. At least 6,000 houses were destroyed by water and hundreds of cars and trucks swept away and lost. Over 1,000 businesses were damaged beyond repair, hundreds of farm animals drowned and 25 people lost their lives. Many terrible losses occurred and the government has estimated the cost in many millions of euros.

and judge how much financial aid the government needs to provide.

I was still in Toronto when the rain began on Sunday afternoon. I received an email from Bob that same day, as he wanted to describe his Sunday morning spent with a group of thirty others, cleaning the Ourne. Usually carried out in April, this event is an annual necessity: to remove, by hand, metal and plastic and glass accumulated over the past months, since proper environmental practices are largely unobserved in rural France and trash is often dumped on the banks of streams.

Divided into pairs, the group worked together for two hours before the rain started, and in that time collected many garbage bags of junk. Bob's partner, a fellow named Denis, was pleased to share his passion for the Scottish writer Robert Louis Stevenson and his nineteenth-century classic, *Travels with a Donkey in the Cévennes*. He told Bob that his family has traced itself back to the fourteenth century, and that they've never left the Cévennes except for a few who moved to Nîmes and some others who fled the country during the wars of religion. He promised that he would bring his family tree to Mas Blanc sometime so that Bob could see it.

However, rain began to fall so heavily that work was stopped and the picnic lunch was held indoors at a nearby *foyer rural*. Glasses of pastis were rapidly downed and food eaten quickly as the downpour continued unabated. Nevertheless, the mood was merry and Bob felt welcome and—more strongly than ever—absolutely *chez lui*.

Shortly after he returned to Mas Blanc and sent the email, the power went off. He lit glass oil-lamps bought in Belleville years ago and got a blaze going in the fireplace. But by nightfall the intensity of the storm had increased, and what had begun as an old-fashioned lamp-lit evening turned into something distinctly unpleasant and deeply frightening.

When I arrived on Wednesday, two days after the storm, I knew about the flood from television in Toronto but had no real notion how seriously the region—or our corner of it—had been affected. But I took note that Bob, who had come to Montpellier to meet me, looked drawn and shaken, not his usual steady, cheerful self. Slowly, as we drove through the ravaged countryside, he provided details and I began to understand what he had been through—and what suffering had occurred all around us.

"The bridge across the Ourne is half gone," he said, to start his report. "I got out by the track around the vineyards when they finally cleared it this morning. We haven't had water or power or the telephone since Sunday night, and I expect it's going to take some time to get the lines up again." He laughed, seeing my face register the news: this meant no email. That meant *serious* deprivation.

"You'll see, as we get up past Quissac," he said, "the vineyards are a disaster. The *vendange* was supposed to start on the weekend but they can't pick now, the vines are covered with mud and the grapes are ruined. And everyone was saying that it was going to be an excellent year after such a long hot summer."

We would not drive through Sommières as we usually do, he explained, as roads were washed out. We took another route, but it did nothing to disguise the consequences of the flood. From trees and shrubs and fences along the road, scraps of plastic fluttered like the tattered flags of a defeated army. Cars and vans, windshields wrapped by flood-swept grass, sat stupidly by the roadside and in the middle of fields, looking as stunned as if they'd just understood the term *write-off*.

"The sound of it, that's what I can't get out of my head," Bob said, after he'd parked our car by the barn and we made our way down to the Ourne, clear and lovely in its forgetfulness. "The noise was deafening and kept getting louder during the night. And of course the louder it was, the closer I knew the water was to the house. And in the dark. . . ." He stopped, and I imagined how terrifying it must have been.

He had taken a flashlight out on the terrace, but it was hard to see through the sheets of rain, and the funnel of light only showed a circle of rushing foam. As the river rose and the tumult increased, there was no way to know when it would stop, or where. He set the alarm clock every half hour in case he should fall asleep, but there was no need, as adrenalin and the noise kept him awake.

Around five in the morning a huge wall of water came down the valley when the dam above the Gour de l'Oule collapsed under the weight of the swollen river. It was this enormous wave that created the worst havoc—taking with it, as it rushed through, everything it could possibly take: the stone bridge, our trees, Haddou's tractor, everything.

Although the cost of rebuilding the wall and re-installing the septic system will be steep—around twenty thousand euros—at least part will be financed by our insurance. Haddou, on the other hand, may never recuperate his losses, for insurance replaces what was destroyed, but it does not upgrade. His old tractor was worth almost nothing, but without it, then what? The scraps of this and that with which he'd made his chicken coop and garden sheds—no value, but how to make these things again? As for his chickens and ducks and geese and rabbits, all of them disappeared but for one large duck who returned the same day I did. She has taken up residence on a new sandy shoal at the bottom of the garden. Her dark brown feathers gleaming in the sunshine, she spends her day preening and swimming in circles as if nothing untoward has occurred. Watching her, I feel such shame, remembering that not so long ago I wished Haddou would clean his yard—now, there is nothing to clean.

Bob and I stand on the bare rocks and look around, both of us aghast at what we see. Even though we are safe, this terrible flood has made us feel vulnerable to the next one, as next there will no doubt be. When we first came to Mas Blanc, we could hardly see the Ourne through the trees and the tall reeds and grass—it was, in North American terms, "just a crick." Now that same ribbon of water is deep and wide, for the moment at least; and its sloping banks of rubble and rock seem to come right up to the house.

As we are examining the property, we see Haddou at his end of the Mas, and we go over to talk. He tells us that his wife, Malika, is still in the hospital, for since the night of the flood her heart has been fibrillating at an excessive rate. Not until two days had passed could they get her out for medical attention. She was very frightened, he says, and drops his head down in a gesture suggesting that he too experienced fear. You had good luck not to be here, he tells me and I nod, at a loss for words. Later, I send over roast chicken and lemon cake to welcome Malika home, but there is nothing anyone can do to bring back Haddou's garden.

Bob and I walk down the field along the stream and see that, apart from breaking along the top at one side, the old dam that created our private swimming place has withstood the pressure. But, dam or not, there's no longer any secret green bower, for the trees beside the stream have been washed away—along with half our fruit trees. Look on the bright side, we tell each other, the other half were spared, along with the olive grove. Huge bundles of grass and twigs have wrapped themselves around what few trees remain as if in agony, hanging on for dear life; gravel and boulders are spread across the road and the field, metal fence-posts are bent in half, and the sign to our house is half buried in fallen trees and bushes. It is a mess. We can see that we have a lot of work ahead of us, but we promise we will not complain, for everyone else along this valley has been similarly affected. What our neighbours say is true: we are all in this together.

Just as Bob began the day of the flood in a spirit of solidarity, he found that same sense of community a day later, when the waters finally receded but Mas Blanc was still cut off from the main road. As night was falling, Denis and his teenage son arrived at the door, having come across the vineyard by foot, carrying a big thermos of drinking water, a container of stew, a loaf of bread, apples, cake and chocolate— and a photocopied document showing Denis's entire family tree.

After two days at home, I drive into Anduze to see for myself the devastation caused by the Gardon ripping through the narrow streets. Receding, the river deposited thick, dirty sand, and the normally neat little village looks foul and defiled. Everywhere, doors are open to air the damp interiors, and outside these doors are piles of soiled clothes, sodden mattresses, muddied books, broken things—ruined stuff. It has all become *stuff*. There's melancholy in the air like a sad song: the scene resembles a medieval allegorical painting, the intent of which is to teach us that possessions are nothing but vanity and that all earthly things decay.

I find only one *boulangerie* open; the others have had their ovens ruined. The small supermarket where we regularly do our shopping was flooded to the ceiling and is most definitely closed. Le Petit Jardin is closed until further notice, with a heavy black line drawn about a metre from the ground beside the doorway: the high-water mark. Shop after shop, closed.

Nevertheless, people seem in good humour. For one thing, the sun is shining again. For another, there are teams of men sweeping the streets in an amazingly efficient manner. Everyone is working together to clean up the dried mud, for Anduze depends on tourism and cannot afford these unsightly conditions. Fortunately, the busy summer season has just ended: everyone, in discussing the flood, mentions this as *bonne chance*—the tragedy would have been far more serious if tourists had still been in the many large campsites by the river.

In season, Anduze caters to thousands of visitors from northern Europe, offering an array of antique stores and boutiques selling the usual regional crafts: lavender sachets, olivewood bowls, beeswax candles, colourful pottery and glass. More recently, new shops have sprung up displaying Indian jewellery and incense, Chinese silk scarves, Thai cotton tunics, African masks and Peruvian flutes—that peculiar combination of merchandise accompanying tourism like a camp follower around the world.

As I walk up the cobblestone street to the central marketplace, I see a woman hauling boxes and racks of clothing from a shop that opened last June. I had noticed then that her merchandise had an Asian motif—Indonesian sarongs and a style of woven baskets I remembered from the Philippines—and although I intended to look inside never did so before leaving for Canada. Today, I say *bonjour* and a word or two of sympathy, as it is obvious that her floor space had been flooded—but what stops me in my tracks is a row of muddy-footed Bul-ul pots outside her door. Exactly like the ones Antoine gave us years ago, these black brooding figures with empty crowns sit waiting to be filled with flowers.

"*Madame,*" I begin, without polite preliminaries, "*est-ce que vous avez obtenu ces pots des Philippines . . . de Banaue?*"

She stops lugging her rack onto the street, and smiles. Yes, she says, that's exactly where they came from, and they're on sale now, end of the season.

I reply that we already have two sitting outside our house, and that I am interested to know how she obtained them, as we had once known a man in Banaue, a Frenchman in fact, who taught a group of teenage boys to make pots like these. Maybe these have come from the same workshop? Would she have an address for her Filipino supplier?

Her expression changes, only slightly. My connection, she says, is here. It is my friend who goes back and forth and who supervises the making of the pots. I can give you his name and number. And with that she writes a telephone number on a slip of paper, and the name: Antoine.

He lives in Sauve—a village not far from Latourne—and he has been there nearly three years, she tells me, dividing his time between France and the Philippines. I explain that we will be without our telephone for at least another week, I wonder if I might go directly to visit him. Easy, she says, he runs a little craft shop in the centre of the village, and he lives above it. She gives me directions and I thank her profusely, trying to impress upon her how astonishing this coincidence seems.

The next day I drive to Sauve, on the banks of the Vidourle, a river so famous for its flooding that there's a name for it: *vidourlade*. During the years we lived in Montpellier, this quaint medieval village made an ideal afternoon outing when Canadian friends came to visit: not only was it ancient, authentic and slightly mysterious, but its hillside setting by the swan-spotted river was highly picturesque, the tall narrow buildings crowded against each other in a charming jumble. Now that we live only a stone's throw away, I never go to Sauve: I find its narrow streets too dark and depressing, the ambiance more grim than enchanting.

Without difficulty, as the village is small and the directions are clear, I find Antoine's craft shop situated on a very pleasant square edged with plane trees that does not conform to my gloomy impression of Sauve. I ring the bell to his apartment above the shop and tell the Filipino child who calls down from the window that I am an old friend from the Philippines and give her my name. She lets me in, and I go up two flights of stone stairs, wondering if he will remember me or I him. It has been a very long time.

Although his moustache is no longer ragged but stylish, and his clothing elegant rather than shabby, Antoine himself has not changed much—and it would seem neither have I, as we recognize each other on sight. He recalls photographs I sent him of Melchior and Sarah, taken the day we met in Banaue in 1993. No longer infants, they're thirteen and eleven, joined by an adopted sister named Melanie, who is eight; all three are beautiful, happy-looking children. Antoine says they have lots of friends in Sauve and have fitted in well—this is evident as we watch Melchior tear around the square with several other boys in a game of tag. My view of the village suffers a final reversal during the afternoon, as I see what fun it must be to play in these twisting streets, and as I hear from Antoine how secure he feels as a parent in such a safe and close-knit community.

As he did in Banaue, Antoine serves tea and although he is coughing with the *grippe* allows himself a cigarette; as we talk, it all feels very familiar, as if I am visiting an old friend. He tells me that he left the Philippines not long after we did, to study law in Bordeaux. After that, a year in Montpellier, during which a chance trip with friends to Sauve—*par hasard,* he says—convinced him it would be a good place to bring up his children.

Back in Banaue, all goes well. The other children are grown and independent, he makes regular trips to see them and to bring back items he sells in Sauve. He has put aside plans for an active career in law until he passes another set of exams, which he will do in a year or two. In the meantime, he volunteers his services to an anti-globalization organization and to other local groups who can benefit from his knowledge of the law.

We arrange that he will bring the children over to Mas Blanc for a meal, after the flood damage has been repaired and the outdoor area is entirely safe again. As I leave his apartment and head out of the village, the autumn sunshine shifts and shimmers across the countryside, and on the hills ahead the light catches the broken stone walls of abandoned mulberry terraces stepping in straight lines up the slope. I wonder if Antoine and the children have been struck, as I have, by the coincidence of coming to live among terraces.

Seeing Antoine has brought back with great force the phrase he used when we met: if your desire is rooted in your heart, then everything is possible. It's good to keep such optimism in mind when there is so much to do. Fortunately, within a few days we have power and the telephone again. We call Jamal, who comes immediately. Later that week, he and Nazim arrive with a mechanical shovel to reinstall the septic system, and we are able to use the indoor plumbing again. They present us with plans for a concrete wall and promise they will make it as soon as they can. We don't even joke about the usual dodge *"normalement,"* as we know we are high on their list of priorities now. Over a beer at the end of the day, Nazim tells us about his brother and sister-in-law who, from the safety of higher ground, watched their house get swallowed up in the flood and saw everything they owned disappear into the churning water. We stand in silence, out by the barn, thinking about how awful it would be to lose everything.

"What is the loss they find hardest to bear?" I ask, framing a reply to the question in my head, imagining the heartbreak—knowing that my tears would be shed not over large items but small. The hardest would be the loss of all those little things that surround you with their silent stories of who you are, stories you tell yourself over and over: the basket of pretty stones, the china bowl of seashells, the box of saved letters, the album of family photographs. The small glass bird, the jar of pearl buttons you keep on your desk. If all these were swept away forever, would you still remember, would you still have your stories?

"La perte de souvenirs," says Nazim, as if reading my mind. I understand that he does not mean the loss of holiday souvenirs manufactured to evoke place; he means those objects around us that hold and guard our memories, that tell our stories. We are lucky, Bob and I. We did not lose our souvenirs. In a flash, I realize—gratitude mixed with amazement—how much I love Mas Blanc. It is already filled with memory, the house itself my souvenir. Who could have predicted this slow flood of love taking over my heart?

Later, I talk to Bruno, whose section of Mas Blanc was flooded from water running down the road that passes along the hillside. He has opened his windows and emptied his rooms to dry them out and has begun to repair his tile roof—but has left that work for later, for he has another, more pressing priority: he is appearing for several nights in a benefit performance to raise money for flood victims in nearby Alès. Typical, I think. The house will always come last, and the essentials will always come first: doing what makes him happy and doing good for others, more often than not the same thing.

However, conversations about the flood have a depressing effect as days pass, as does the dreary reality that we have an enormous amount of physical work to do in the weeks ahead. I revert to self-protective habit one morning after breakfast and go to the *Books of Knowledge,* finding consolation in these old books as I always have: reading my grandmother's encyclopedia has long been my way to restore my equilibrium. My normal method is to pick a book at random out of the twenty, and then leaf through until I find "The Book of Wonder," the section in which Arthur Mee, self-styled Wise Man, answered children's questions about the world. His tone—self-consciously arch, condescending and overtly Christian—might make another reader cringe: but his is the magic voice from my childhood, the Wise Man who always had the answer. Today I open to a section devoted to the question of time.

> Whatever we call now, whether we call it six o'clock or twelve o'clock, this now is now everywhere. The present moment is the present moment here and on the farthest star. It would be foolish of us to make a mystery where none exists, or to forget that now must be now everywhere. Thus, the answer to the question, "where does the day begin?" is that the day is always beginning somewhere.

The hugeness of it. The thrilling, brain-aching hugeness of it, this notion overwhelmed me when I first read these lines. "Now is everywhere, and all the time." The notion of the day beginning in every moment carried with it—although it didn't say so in the book—the fact that it was ending in every moment too. It would be another dozen years before I would encounter T. S. Eliot's *Four Quartets,* and until then, I felt as if Mee and I were among a handful of people in the world who understood what was going on.

I sit on the terrace with the book on my lap and look across to the vineyards marching off toward St-Baudile, and down to the rocky beach that used to be the garden. It seems that time is showing me its many faces, and I can see them all at once. The creep of time and the run of it, the flash of sun on water and the quicksilver glint of fish in the deep, the wind pulling at the poplars until leaves unhook themselves and spin down like gold coins in the air. The little Ourne, grown thuggish with power and ruining the landscape like some mad bully, has now shrunk back into a sweet spinster who would not dream of making waves. The ghost of Heraclitus rises from the water, reminding me that I am a river too. We are all just passing through.

There is no such thing as time, says the Wise Man. There is only change.

Even before the septic system has been fully repaired, I risk doing a wash: a week of rain is predicted but today is sunny and windy, perfect weather for drying clothes on the line. As I stand there pinning wet shirt-tails to each other with plastic pegs, I look down and feel relieved that the small flat stone marking Ballou's grave was undisturbed by the flood. At this end of the property, two old oaks have wound their roots so solidly into the ground that they saved this corner of the stone wall from being washed away. Only two metres along, there is nothing but exposed soil, and beyond that, bare rock.

There will be no morels for Hervé to pick on this section of the Ourne next spring, no wild asparagus and iris and narcissus along its banks. And there will be fewer frogs to serenade us through the summer nights, for the millpond in which they sang has been destroyed; the water system the pond was part of no longer exists, and the stone aqueduct across the river is badly broken. It will be months, perhaps years before all is made right again.

It is a perfect September morning, clear and fresh. Until now, thick foliage made a leafy sound-barrier between us and the stream below, but since the flood everything green has gone, and what I see from here is bright flashing water falling over white rock and what I hear is the splashing noise of water falling. The view has completely changed, and—this is the shock—it is beautiful. It is, possibly, even more beautiful than it was before. Below the rocks I look down into a deep turquoise pool—next summer, it will be a swimming hole par excellence.

Standing here by the clothesline, I can see for the first time all the way down to the arches of the broken bridge—where it collapsed there's a lazy slant, as if the bridge has given up and gone to sleep. The mayor of Latourne has told us that it may be months before it is repaired, for there are many more important bridges than ours to fix. Looking down the field toward our ruined orchard and all the fallen trees along the river, I envisage the work that we must do in order to get on with our lives. There are mornings with the chainsaw and the shovel and the wheelbarrow ahead of us, evenings of sore muscles and aching backs. But it seems the river has opened up the land in an astonishing way. I can see where I am more clearly than ever before.

S.E.M.A.P.H.O.R.E.

THIS STORY LIES BETWEEN true and not true.

Like many other little girls growing up in the 1940s and '50s, I was a Brownie, delighting in the chummy, clubby rituals of skipping around the toadstool and the orderliness of lining up to show our clean hands and shiny shoes. Later, when we flew up to the higher realm of Girl Guides, we were introduced to more serious pursuits in the hope that one day we'd be all-round citizens, just as capable and courageous as Boy Scouts and, like them, able to start a campfire without matches.

We believed this would be true. We believed that we strong, able and clever girls would rule the planet with our crucial new accomplishments, we who now knew all manner of essential, self-preserving skills, our badges sewn neatly onto our sleeves to prove our worth. But in truth, we had entered a male domain, dictated by rules and codes of behaviour that kept us locked in a feverish, urgent race to get as many badges as we could. It was all about winning, that's what I remember. Competition among the sixes, achievement measured by best or last, a sick feeling in the pit of your stomach when you turned up without your project done. Test after test after test to see who would be first—tying knots, knitting washcloths, identifying trees, making porridge over an open fire.

And semaphore.

In order to be a full-fledged Girl Guide, you had to get your badge in semaphore. That is, you had to be able to send messages by flag across large bodies of water. Seems laughable now, but we took it seriously then, for none of us questioned the value of such knowledge; we simply learned what we were taught. We were good girls and we did what we were told in order to get the next badge. In fact, knots and trees and porridge and fire connected us sensibly to the world, but semaphore, even then, was a relic from another time for which we would never find a use—unless, by chance, one of us in later life might find herself on a stranded yacht and become the handy heroine who saves the hapless crew.

Nevertheless, in the small Guide troop to which I belonged, once a week over one long winter we mem-orized the moves, and when we did the tests to see how well we'd learned, we stood at one end of the

gymnasium with our back to the receiver of the message so that not even a vowel could be transmitted by
rolling eye or twitching lip.

"Too tempting to give the flags your face," said Mrs.
Whittington, our grey-haired captain who had been in
the war and who liked to say that *she* knew what was
what. She seldom left a stone unturned in her search—
not for perfection, but for faults: she was of the old
school, believing children were, at heart, amoral creatures to be watched at all times for signs of inherent
guile. Never mind that we were reading the signals
from behind the sender, not as it would have happened
had we truly been on the receiving end—all that mattered to Mrs. Whittington was that we had no occasion
to deceive her. "Girl Guides never cheat," she'd say,
while staring at us hard with squinty eyes.

The scene I am remembering, in the middle of
Canada in the middle of the last century in the middle
of the winter, unrolls like old film, grainy and shadowy
but for the magpie flags. There we are, two dozen girls
in dark blue cotton dresses, preparing for the day when
we might be marooned at sea. With slender, girlish
arms churning like choppy windmills, we signalled
H.E.L.P. all right, we signalled I. A.M. H.E.R.E. We
signalled I. K.N.O.W. W.H.O. Y.O.U. L.O.V.E. I.T.
I.S. S.M.E.L.L.Y. B.I.L.L.Y. H.A. H.A.

Our arms suddenly hands, we told our letters by the
clock, quarter to five, ten after six, winding words

around us in the air. Flags in fists, we stood stock-still with winter-itchy legs we couldn't scratch for danger of misspelling, and with bits of cloth on sticks told imaginary ships across imaginary water that we were not the enemy—but who were they? F.R.I.E.N.D. O.R. F.O.E? We asked and asked, until we got it right.

Our small uniformed bodies becoming poems, we waved ourselves out of girlhood and into the next invisible chapter where words would mean or not mean because of whose lips or hands upon our skin would tell us L.O.V.E., would tell us D.A.N.G.E.R., would tell us G.O.O.D.B.Y.E. We became our own language, we learned from the body what words could do when they could not be spoken and only guessed from across the room.

I think I can still do it, you know. Can still stand up and take a position befitting any letter—kinetic memory makes the body metaphor. I am alphabet, or more, with all these words in my bones and blood. I am Alpha and Omega, the beginning and the end, Goddess of Language with flags for a tongue. And now my arms and wrists remember the letter *S* and that long-ago March night we played forbidden lights-out tag while waiting for Mrs. Whittington who, for some unaccountable reason—it had never happened before—was late.

We raced around the darkened gymnasium, some of us hiding behind the curtains on the small raised stage at one end of the room. And *S* is for my friend Sharon who fell in that pitch-black place, and *S* is for her Scream when she fell and then her Silence. Suddenly, overhead lights were flicked on by some girl near the switch and then we saw the bright blood pouring from Sharon's throat, her terrified eyes, her face draining of colour. No one knew what to do, we had not yet come to badges in Emergency First Aid, but someone held a scarf to Sharon's neck as she gasped for air. And then we heard the siren of the ambulance. One of the older girls had had the presence of mind to run out of the school and across to a house to phone for H.E.L.P.

Whose fault? Our captain wanted to know. Whose idea was the game of tag? No one remembered. None of us would take or pass the blame and we shared it among us, one enormous pool of wordless guilt. We were mute. As was Sharon, in the hospital where we were not allowed to go, as the age limit for visitors was twelve and many of us were not that old. We sent her cards, and bouquets, and comic books and jokes, but when some of the older Guides went to see her, they reported that she turned her face and would not look at them or smile.

For weeks she stayed in the hospital, and then, finally, she came home, with a little metal plate at the base of her throat and a sort of rubber-hose hole in it, which made a breathy, squeezing sound when she tried to talk.

She would never have a voice again, only this embarrassing sound of squashed wind, of awful sorrow. We were all so sorry for Sharon, each of us feeling it must have been *our* fault, with the terrible eyes of Mrs. Whittington drilling into our souls.

She had cut her throat against the edge of a metal folding chair. Who could have known it was there? Who could have known she would fall? No one. But still, guilt ran through us like a stream of poison and worse, the thought: it could have been me, but it wasn't. And with that came an enormous wash of relief rushing through our wicked, unwounded bodies.

When Girl Guides began again that autumn, after having been cancelled in March "until further notice," we were a chastened lot. None of us wanted to be in that gymnasium again, but our mothers said we must. They said that life goes on, that we'd be glad someday. Sharon came back too, white-faced and grim and silent. We'd hardly seen her during the summer, and she came to school only now and again, as if the effort of rejoining all of us healthy girls was just too much for her to bear. It was true, what the older girls had said, she refused to smile at all. Meaning to cheer her up a bit, I said, "Well anyway, Share, you were always the best at semaphore, so let's get the old flags out!" and touched her shoulder in a friendly way. I liked her and I hated seeing her sad.

She made a little rasping sound out of her voicebox, and as tears flew from her eyes all the other girls gathered round and stared. They told Mrs. Whittington what I'd said to make Sharon cry, and she declared I'd been needlessly hurtful and asked me to leave immediately. "Guides are never thoughtless and never cruel," she said. I tried to explain that I had meant to make Sharon feel better, I'd meant to make her smile, but she just kept looking at me in that hard, awful way and told me to go home, she'd call my parents later in the evening.

I walked home along the leaf-strewn streets in the lamp-lit dark, bewildered by how easy it was to make mistakes and vowing I would never speak again myself. I too would clam up forever. Fearful, ashamed and sorry for hurting Sharon. And angry at being not heard, at being so badly misunderstood.

All these decades later, those feelings have flagged themselves into the present. Curious and bewildered by what I am remembering, I write it down . . . and from Sharon's injured throat there springs a story of silence, a way of telling what it is to lose your voice.

Fabricating this tale out of memory, at first I believe I am in control—but slowly I understand that it is the story deciding where it comes from and how it goes. Mrs. Whittington emerges out of the shadows of the unconscious and become herself—she, who never existed, who comes to life solely for the purposes of plot. The Girl Guides stand in obedient lines, as real as they ever were, silently waving their semaphore flags and waiting for disaster. Implicit now is the hope that Sharon forgave and forgives.

Winding its way back into the mysterious dark, the story found what wanted to come forward into the light: that long, sweet moment of hiding, before Sharon fell.

Stories

THE WINDOW

Her husband calls Lila down from her study, where she is rereading *Mansfield Park,* to join him on the front terrace. She has finally agreed, after much discussion, to refer to this recently rebuilt structure of cement, tile and brick as the *front* terrace, because it is occasionally necessary in conversation to differentiate it from the other terrace at the back of the house: *south* and *north* had sounded too posh, as if the place were larger and grander than it is, and *her* preferred term—porch—was rejected because porches, like verandas, are meant to be made of wood, her husband said. She gave in graciously, but she never actually calls it the front terrace: she simply doesn't say *porch* anymore. Of such small compromises are happy marriages made, and as she goes down the stairs and out the front door to where he is waiting, she is smiling, thinking this. She loves John so much that it does not seem too much trouble to avoid foolish arguments about this word or that.

He often calls her down at the end of an evening to come out to see how clear the night sky is, or to watch the moon rising over the roof. He takes a childlike pleasure in the fact that they live out in the country now, where urban illumination cannot spoil the stars. He has spent the greater part of his life in cities, and retirement to this old stone house on the edge of a vineyard is a continuing source of satisfaction for him: stargazing together is simply another way of being glad that life has turned out as it has, and she knows this as she stands with her head turned up heavenward and her neck aching, eyes focused on one constellation or another. They live in another country than the one they are from, and it is a great comfort to her that the sky map is recognizable.

But this time the call is to sit on the terrace wall and look back into the house through the oblong eight-paned window that gives a view of the dining room inside. The room is golden and glowing, lit in some way that makes it seem something other than reality: a painting, a photograph. Lila is immediately struck by this idea and says so to John, who replies that this is exactly why he called her down. "I thought it looked like a painting too," he says, "and I knew

you'd want to see it. Dutch, do you think? Maybe
seventeenth century?"

He's right, she agrees, for all kinds of reasons: the
window frame, the contrast between light and shadow
and of course the yellow tulips arranged loosely in a
pottery jug in the centre of the bare cedar table,
directly under the old hanging lamp with its shade of
crocheted string. Both the shade and the jug were gifts
from friends, and she marvels at how their sentimental
histories are diminished by their visual importance.
Who needs to know the name of the man who gave
her the Italian jug more than three decades ago? All
that matters is the colour of the glaze—the top half
mustard and the bottom ochre—a perfect complement
to the wooden surface of the table gleaming in the
lamplight the colour of wild honey, and to the tulips,
which are pale rosy-yellow, nearly translucent, seeming to shine from within themselves.

She knows that if she were to come across this
picture—painting or photograph—in some glossy
magazine, she would clip it immediately and pin it
on the bulletin board above her writing desk, as a
daily reminder that beauty exists in the world. She
would probably feel some envy of whoever lived in
such a house, and she would, if she had the time,
allow her mind to roam around the picture, picking
out details upon which her curiosity and imagination could work. *What kind of people would live in*

*such a place? What else is there in the room that I
can't see?*

The tulips, she notes, seem to be doing a wild kind
of dance, reaching out crazily from the jug as if daring
each other to see how far they can lean and not fall.
Some of them are full-blown, for she bought them at
the market Wednesday and it is now Sunday: even
with a small brass coin in the water, guaranteed by the
flower seller to keep their green stems straight, they
began to bend and curve after a few days, opening up
in bawdy fashion to show their black stamens and
bright orange pistils. She notices too how there are two
different kinds of light in the room: the direct glare of
the bulb on the tulips and the table, and the soft radiance filtering through the tiny holes of the crocheted
shade. Out on the terrace, there's a cloudy darkness
overhead the colour of bruises, or ripe blue plums, and
not one star interferes with her delight in the window.

"But isn't it absurd," she says, turning away into
the darkness, "that when we come across something
as perfect as this we say it is like art, and if it *were* art
we'd appreciate it by saying how like life it is?"

"That's why I called you down, Lila," he says. "So
you could deliver one of your fine lectures on aesthet-
ics." He says this in a kindly way, his joking tone bred
of long familiarity: they've been married for nearly
twenty years, a second marriage for both. Although
he would not presume to predict her reactions (having

sometimes done so and learned it is always unwise), most of her responses will be pretty much within a range, and he feels safe enough on this ground. Her favourite topic is always art: what it means, why we have it, could we do without it, is it a meaningful manifestation of the human spirit—Lila can find a way to manage any conversation and turn it round until art is at its core. And she does (she admits this) tend to become a little didactic, once she gets going: she was a schoolteacher for too many years, she says, and she can't help it.

"You're teasing," she says, moving over to lean against him so that their two bodies are wedged together in one big cosy shape. They've both gained a few pounds since John retired from Foreign Affairs and they moved to this house, but neither of them minds particularly. "Don't think I don't know it. But I'm so pleased to be looking at this window I don't care one bit. Tease away."

He pulls her a little closer, and as he does so she is aware of a peculiar shift within her, as if two parts of her self have come apart: one stays here with him, her slightly overweight and grey-haired husband to whom she is enormously grateful for knowing her so well and calling her down. She feels his physical presence warm and comforting, she knows the flesh beneath his knitted cotton pullover as intimately, as completely, as she knows her own.

But strangely, another part of her self goes flinging off into space, whizzing about like a firecracker without any aim or sense. She has suddenly left him, and left the window, and is somewhere out there in the dark, looking down on the terrace from above, as if she is standing outside another frame looking in at another picture. She has the dizzying sensation that everything in human experience is framed, and every step we take is either into, or out of, one of these frames. It seems a horrifyingly private epiphany she will never be able to explain, and she knows she's going to have to swallow it, like so much else that goes on wordlessly in her head, and simply absorb it into her silent self. Sometimes it seems to Lila that she will explode from all that's unsaid inside her and she wonders: *What is it that I want to say?*

The name of the man who gave her the Italian pottery jug was Warren. She brings her mind back from abstraction with the clear memory of this name, and of the man himself: Warren Bundles. His name had always struck her as funny, hilarious even, particularly because he had been a tall, angular fellow and those two names together, Warren and Bundles, resonated with images of little furry animals in warm burrows, or perhaps rose-breasted barn swallows in their nests. She'd been very fond of him, had slept with him for two or three months, but even naked and intimate in the tumbled sheets of his bed could never summon

the courage to ask if he was embarrassed by his
name, had ever thought of changing it, and if he
would, to what?

At this very moment the telephone in the living
room rings, and she has the unsettling notion that it
will be Warren, even though she knows full well he
has been dead many years, a car accident in New
Jersey, freak snowstorm, awful. She loosens herself
from John's warm grip and says, "I'll go. It'll probably
be one of the kids." They share five between them
(two hers, two his and one theirs) who frequently call
at odd hours, neglectful of the time difference
between their parents' home and their own. As she
walks into the glow of the dining room, she looks
again at the jug as she passes the table and feels
washed all over, as if the light is golden water. She
sees in memory poor, dead Warren, sees him as he
was the day he gave the jug to her—he'd gone to
Siena to a conference and brought it back as proof
he'd been thinking of her.

She'd grown sure, while he was away, that she did
not care for him as he seemed to care for her, and
she'd been rehearsing how she might tell him this
when he returned. And there he was at the door of
her apartment, pushing a wrapped box into her hands
and bending to kiss her at the same time, saying, "I
hope you like this, it's very typical of the region." She
could laugh out loud even now, remembering that

line, and the eager awkward kiss slightly off to the side and including half her nose. She had laughed because she could not help laughing. She was a small woman, freckled and fair and softly round, seeming unconsciously to exude on any and all difficult occasions gentle and genuine forgiveness for either insult or injury. But the kiss fell into neither category—it was simply badly placed and deserved a good laugh.

They'd broken up soon after that, and she had given him back a string of pearls he'd given her at Christmas. They weren't real pearls, but it seemed such a personal gift that she felt she must do the decent thing, in case he felt that by keeping the pearls she was somehow still attached to him and not perfectly serious about breaking up. After all, she'd begun the process by telling him she hadn't missed him when he was in Italy. But she didn't give him back the pottery jug. She rather liked it, but that wasn't the reason she kept it so much as it seemed that by returning it she'd cast a sour shadow not only on his taste in pottery but on his remembrance of Siena, when he had been happy and had still thought she might love him.

So she kept it and he kept the tie and the pen and the scarf that she'd given him, and they parted with dignity and few tears. From time to time she heard of him—they'd shared a wide circle of friends, one of whom had introduced them and who never gave up hoping they'd get back together—but she hadn't seen him for many years at the time of his death, couldn't even imagine what he must have looked like by then. Poor Warren was gone, and there remained only the jug, which had followed her ever since, how many years? She met and married her first husband, Nick, shortly after their breakup, and that had been thirty-four years ago.

John's daughter Kate had once asked for the pottery jug when she was rooting through the house looking for stuff she could take to furnish a new flat, and Lila had felt a bit mean-spirited, refusing to let her have it, but really, if anyone were to have the jug it should be Jessica, her own daughter who'd grown up with this thing holding flowers or milk or just sitting dusty on the sideboard. But Jessica has become a radical activist living the sort of existence in which something like a jug belonging to her mother would be more than a burden—it would be a symbol of all that must be smashed. Jessica had not asked for anything even when she went off on her own at eighteen, and has been known to send back birthday or Christmas cheques with a small note suggesting that Lila send this amount to some worthwhile organization: Greenpeace, Earthroots, Oxfam.

The phone call is from Tommy, John's son who is now at Cornell doing a post-doc. He's never really lived with Lila and his father, although he has a warm

and civil relationship with them both: still, she feels
no flutter of parental desire to hear his voice when he
calls, pleased though she is that he's calling his father.
Within a few beats—the brief exchange of step-
mother and stepson—she has said, "Listen, sweet-
heart, your dad's right here out on the terrace, you
know how he loves to look at the stars. Hold on, I'll
get him."

Lila re-enters the room of shining gold just as John
comes toward her, with an intuitive sense that the call
is probably for him. He's been expecting Tommy to
phone with news of whether his grant has come
through for the Galapagos. As they pass each other at
the end of the table John stops her for an instant,
bending to kiss the part in her sandy-grey hair. "*Front*
terrace, darling," he says. "You just said *terrace*."

Lila pulls away enough to punch his chest in a fairly
firm manner. "You're a despot," she says with a
laugh, unwinding herself from his embrace. As he
moves into the darkness of the unlit living room to
pick up the phone, she turns and walks out the front
door again, to stand looking back through the window. What might she have missed in that first look?
Could she paint this picture now, herself? She's been
taking lessons from a retired professor of art from
Bath who lives in a nearby village. Recently, the class
has been working at *composition,* and Lila has found it
immensely satisfying to practise this new way of

looking at the world, always measuring a scene in terms of what to leave out and what to include. Here, the tulips, the jug, the table, the lamp and the frame of the eight-paned window. So simple. More an illustration than a painting, but an illustration for what?

Lila sits on the terrace wall, listening to the sounds of the night—the frogs began to honk a week or two ago, proof that spring has come. The noise of their croaking seems amplified by the low cloud blocking out the stars and whatever moon there might have been. She can hear her husband's voice now and again but can't catch what he's saying—doesn't matter, he'll give her a full report when the call is finished, he usually makes notes whenever he's talking to any of the kids. She tries now to look in the window and *not* think of Warren Bundles, and to focus on remembering the woman who made the lampshade, or the woman from whom she bought the tulips at the market.

But it's impossible. She has been drawn back into the past and she is filled with regret that Warren is dead and that she cannot, after John is off the line, pick up the phone and call him. "H'lo, Warren? It's Lila calling, I know it's been a very long time, years. . . . No, everything's fine, and you. . . ? Oh, I got your number from the Watsons, I knew they'd have it. . . . Well, it's silly, really, I'm just calling to say you came to mind this evening as I was looking at that vase you gave me. The jug. From Siena."

Would she do this if he were alive? Of course not. Not in a million years. She had never called him once in all the time after . . . well, she wouldn't have wanted him to get the wrong idea, he might have thought she was unhappy in her marriage, making overtures. Yes, she *had* been unhappy with Nick, but it never occurred to her to call Warren, and that's the truth. So now? If she could, would she? No, people don't. People don't go back, they move forward, fish in the stream.

Lila hears John laughing in a hearty way that sounds as if he is winding up the conversation. She continues to look in the window, this time as if she were a spy: what does she see? The cedar table is badly scratched and in need of refinishing. She's been meaning to do this for a long time, and looking through the window now she resolves to put that on her list of things to do, tomorrow. *Table: refinish.*

Her life is framed with lists, most of which end in the wastepaper basket after a day or two. She feels a little uneasy out in the dark, as if her mind is going to loosen itself again and go reeling off into the night and look down fiercely and critically on the rest of her left behind. The sensation is not unpleasant, but she cannot allow it to take her over—she has work to do. She is rereading all of Jane Austen's novels in preparation for writing a review of a new biography, the deadline for which is only a week away. To her surprise, she has rather liked Fanny Price in *Mansfield Park* this time. Previously, she had found her one of Austen's least attractive heroines, too skinny and unhealthy and priggish. Fanny never gives way to a good belly laugh, as Lila herself likes to do. But somehow on this reading she's had increased sympathy for Fanny, always in search of home and never happy where she is.

John has finished his call and stands in the doorway now looking out at his bookish wife who—he can see this, even in the dark—is experiencing some powerful emotion that is making her chin quiver and her eyes shine with tears. He moves rapidly across the terrace toward her and takes her in his arms, folding her up softly against his chest and stroking her hair. "Tommy got the grant," he says, "and he's off for three months, leaving Tuesday. He'll be on board some incredibly high-tech scientific research ship and he's right cockahoop about it. What's the trouble, Lila? Has the window made you upset for some reason?"

"The jug," she manages. "And time, the way it goes. And how to mix the paint to get the right shade of yellow if I were going to paint what I see. And being framed inside frame after frame, and not being able to get out. I'm not sad, darling, I'm only, you know . . . there seems to be much in my head I can't say. And I have to figure out what I'm going to say for this Austen review and my mind is spinning with

memories instead. I think I've been identifying with
Fanny Price so much that I'm feeling homesick and
weepy. Or maybe it's those damn tulips. There's
something horribly sentimental about yellow tulips,
don't you think?" She has delivered this speech into
his chest, and raises her head to look at him, and now
she is smiling. "What do you think?"

John says nothing but gives a short affectionate
laugh and turns her around so that her back is against
him and his arms are wrapped over her breasts. She
leans there, looking back at the window, and he says
nothing. He lets her be silent. And as they stand there
together, quiet in the dark, they become the frame.

ARNICA

For a very long time, Molly and Arthur had wanted to go to Collioure. At last, this past April, they were able to include the picturesque seaside village in their two-week trip to the south of France. Somehow, on earlier visits, they'd never driven that far along the coast: the only time they'd been in the vicinity they had stopped at Perpignan and turned up into the Pyrénées instead. To be honest, seeing Collioure had never been a passionate wish of Molly's: it was Arthur who'd taken it into his head that this was somewhere they both wanted to visit. He was like that, a generous man, who shared everything with Molly, not only his bed and his bank account but even spoonfuls of his *crème brulée* when she refused to order dessert ("you know I'm on a diet, darling"), and his entire life: every thought, dream and aspiration included Molly. He seldom used the first-person pronoun; he began with "we" and ended with "us." Sometimes he couldn't believe he hadn't met Molly until he was over forty, and when, for some reason, he'd be recalling an event from his life before that moment, he would feel bewildered by her absence from the scene.

Arthur had first read about Collioure in a book about French artists, several of whom had spent time there, including Derain and Picasso, and his favourite, Matisse. From the age of twelve, when he visited Paris with his parents for a whirlwind week of sight-seeing, Arthur had been an enthusiastic francophile and over the years had perfected his ability to speak the language so easily that Europeans often took him for one of their own—if not French, definitely Continental. His accent, although clearly of foreign origin, was polished and confident. It gave Arthur inordinate pleasure to set people right, and to tell them that he'd been born and raised in Victoria, British Columbia, Canada. "Not exactly a bastion of francophone culture," he'd say. "But somehow *La Belle France* and I found each other."

Arthur and Molly found each other a few years after he left British Columbia to take up a position teaching statistics in the faculty of social sciences at the University of Ottawa in 1985. He liked his work, and he particularly liked being part of a university where he could use both official languages, French and English. Occasionally he considered a move to some branch of the federal government—his arrival had coincided with a period when bilingual skills were highly prized in the capital, and many of his colleagues had been seduced away by one ministry or another—but in fact Arthur liked the orderly pace of professorial life (the sabbaticals for research, the pressure to publish that kept him on his toes and the flattering flutter of reviews in academic journals) and the sense he had of a secure place within the university and, thus, the world. He cherished his tenure and disliked the idea of making a change, and so he remained where he was.

Molly had been a student—*we're an awful cliché*, they'd tell new friends who didn't know their story— but considerably older than most, as she'd come to university after several years as a secretary—and Arthur had fallen for her "head over heels." Or sometimes he said, "like a ton of bricks." He always used one expression or the other when he spoke of their beginnings, perhaps a bit proudly, as if it proved that beneath his sober vest and tweedy jacket there beat a crazy, passionate heart. Perhaps he *was* a stick-in-the-mud from some points of view, but not when it came to Molly. Within a few months of her appearance at the door of his office (flustered, blushing, her long hair blown around her face in the most becoming disarray) with an overdue essay, he had

initiated proceedings in what turned out to be a bitter and messy divorce from Kay, his wife of twelve
years and the mother of his two children, Wilbur
and Phoebe.

He tried to explain that no one would be happy if
he stayed in the marriage, that they'd all suffer griev-
ous harm to their hearts and souls. But all the children
understood was that Daddy was a monster of selfish-
ness, which is what Kay told them. They moved with
their mother to the west end of the city, where Kay
eventually met a nice-enough real estate agent and
married him: but they never forgave poor Arthur, and
although he tried to re-establish his paternal connection over the years, he failed. Utterly.

Molly had a lot to make up for—loss of family, loss
of face—but unlikely as it seemed to Arthur's friends
and colleagues at the time she married him, she managed to make him very happy. She did it by allowing
him to love her as much as he wanted. They never
had children. Molly put all her energies into her marriage and her part-time job at an NGO: at home she
was adored, and at work appreciated for her intelligence. At Worldword she supervised the sending
of remaindered books overseas to countries where
they might be of some use, and she tried as much
as possible to match up the contents of these crates
of failed books with the recipients to whom they'd
be shipped.

She found this work fascinating, and developed over the years a reputation for being extremely knowledgeable about "development issues" because she followed stories she read in the papers, and always knew the names of education ministers in the countries to which the books were shipped. In the Worldword office there were only four of them, and over time Jerry, Ted and Rhonda had become her best friends. She too thought, now and again, about a move into government, but hated the idea of leaving these people behind. Besides, her French was not fluent, and besides *that*, a career in the public service would be too time-consuming. Arthur came first.

The spring that they went to Collioure was a particularly busy one for Molly and she hated to leave work in April, always a crucial period for Worldword. But since the exam schedule allowed Arthur to get away, and since he had found a very good off-season ticket, Montreal-Nice, she couldn't object. Besides, they were going for only two weeks, and Jerry was quite capable of taking over during her absence. She gave herself almost no time to prepare, threw a few things in a suitcase the day before and that was that. She was in Arthur's hands as far as the arrangements were concerned, a rare turn of events since usually it was she who took charge of planning, getting the best deals for rental cars and making hotel reservations in advance.

"We're going to wing it," said Arthur. "This early in the year we're ahead of the flow, and there's no reason we won't be able to find places to stay if we arrive by mid-afternoon. We're going to take things at a leisurely pace, and just let what happens, happen."

Molly was delighted—on past occasions, Arthur had so often been tense and anxious about the schedules and reservations she had made, wanting everything mapped in advance and then worrying that it wouldn't work out. Too often they'd quarrelled (or worse, not quarrelled, had stayed tight-lipped and quiet), spoiling good meals in restaurants and stalking around cathedrals in such vile temper that they'd missed all manner of important architectural details. Sometimes they'd driven hours in silence, not speaking, as Arthur waited patiently for Molly to regain her senses and as Molly wondered how on God's good earth she had ended up with this tall, thin, peevish man whose neck muscles twitched when he was angry but who never let go and yelled.

But this time, it was going to be different, and in their new, easygoing spirit of laissez-faire they dozed happily across the Atlantic and arrived in Nice in excellent spirits. Indeed, the first few days along the Riviera passed in a blur of good humour: the car they'd rented was a perky little number that imbued both of them with the desire to take the curves along

the Corniche a little faster and tighter than they
would have driven at home.

After an overnight in Montpellier, a city they
had visited twice before and only wanted to stop in
because they loved their little hotel on the rue
Jean-Jacques Rousseau, they drove past Beziers and
stopped in Narbonne, dawdling around the market
beside the canal and sharing a green salad and *quatre
fromages* pizza and carafe of red wine for lunch in the
shadow of the great cathedral.

Finally, late in the afternoon, they found themselves coming down into Collioure itself, the scene
ahead of them utterly familiar from paintings and
photographs: the red-tiled stucco houses on the hillsides, the massive stone walls of the Château Royal at
the foot of the town and the pink domed belltower of
Notre-Dame des Anges at the curve of the beach-
lined harbour. There was even a scattering of brightly coloured fishing boats pulled up on the sand as if
posing for the current generation of painters.
Arthur's enthusiasm could hardly be kept in check,
although of course it expressed itself in the even
tone he used for verifiable statements of fact. "We're
here," he said. "We've done it. We've come to
Collioure at last."

What they hadn't reckoned on was that so far
ahead of the tourist season most of the small hotels
were closed, and the ones that were open were full, so

it took them until sunset to find a suitable place on the
hill road leading to Port-Vendres. The damp-smelling
room had dark maroon wallpaper and framed postcards of Impressionist paintings as decoration, not the
sort of room one spends any time in, but the price was
reasonable and the tall windows opened out over an
elaborate, beautiful garden and in one direction gave a
view of the town curving around its half-moon bay.
Facing in the other direction one looked straight out
to the Mediterranean, which had turned a peculiar
shade of purple as daylight faded. The tide was up,
and waves slashed against the shoreline in dramatic
sprays of white foam.

As they unpacked, they admitted to each other that
the day's driving had tired them both, and agreed
that rather than going in to town now, in the dark,
they'd ask for something light to eat at the hotel, perhaps an omelette, and go to bed early. "We'll be
fresher for a day of walking about," said Arthur.
"And we can read our Michelin tonight and get our
history dates straight again."

They slept fitfully, as during the night the wind
caused one of the wooden shutters to bang incessant-
ly. Arthur got up to fix it, but when he opened the
window to re-do the fastening the cold air rushed in
so fiercely that he was compelled to close the window.
He got back into bed, where he curled himself around
Molly's warm body, and the two of them lay listening

to the rhythmic creak and slam until daybreak, when they fell asleep again.

The morning sun was exceedingly bright when finally they rose and pulled the heavy drapes to look out at the scene before them. Now the sea was brilliant aquamarine, speckled with waves tossing and breaking into streaks of foam. When Arthur opened the window to finally fix the shutter, the air seemed even colder than it had during the night, but he proclaimed it "bracing." Breakfast at the hotel was not included in their rates and, as the omelette the night before had been greasy, they decided to have their coffee in town, where they could buy the papers and relax at a café for a leisurely hour or two. That, of course, was one of the reasons they'd come to Collioure, to sit on the seafront and enjoy the ambiance.

Arthur was particularly looking forward to this part of their stay. The pleasure of being surrounded by the actual background one has seen in paintings: could anything be more satisfying? To be carrying on one's own life—eating, drinking, talking—in the very place a great artist had made immortal by applying paint on canvas! Inexplicable, the thrill, but thrill it was, nonetheless. He looked over at Molly as they walked along down the hill, facing into the wind and swinging their arms vigorously. He thought how enormously happy he was. He felt like a boy again on his first trip to France. He stuck his hands in his pockets and began to whistle his own version of an old Edith Piaf song, which made Molly laugh and attempt to join in, although she'd never learned how to pucker properly and could not produce the sweet clear notes Arthur made so effortlessly.

And then, in an instant, Arthur was no longer walking beside her, but was lying flat, facedown on the sidewalk. There had been whistling in the air, and now there was silence.

Molly told him afterwards she thought that he'd had a stroke, or a heart attack, or been shot by some deranged sniper. She thought that he was dead until, as she bent down, she heard him moan, and as she turned his shoulder to raise his face toward hers, she saw that his forehead had suffered a huge gash and his nose had been badly scraped as well. "Darling, can you speak? Are you okay? What happened?"

As she helped him up to a sitting position, he took his hands from his pockets. "I must have tripped," he said, his voice faint, the breath still knocked out of his lungs. "I tripped on the curb. I couldn't use my arms. . . ." He stopped, and blinked, and for all the world looked like a five-year-old child in spite of his grey moustache. Molly looked back and saw that the road sloped at a discernible angle, and on the side where he'd been walking, the curb was noticeably higher, almost a full step higher. But of course he hadn't been noticing, he'd been looking at her as they were whistling together.

Two women stopped to ask if they could help, and Molly waved them on, saying that everything was fine. But it wasn't fine at all; she felt deeply worried. Might he have suffered a concussion? Should they see a doctor? And as she took tissues from her bag and began to swab his forehead, she saw that there were grains of sand imbedded in the bleeding skin. "We'll go to the pharmacy, darling," she said. "I see a green cross flashing at the end of the street. Look, they'll know what to do. We'll get you fixed up. Can you walk?"

Making their way slowly along the palm-lined walkway of the waterfront, they sensed that they were being observed with interest by everyone who passed. Arthur imagined that he was being regarded as a decrepit old fart given to falling spells, hanging helplessly on the arm of his pretty young wife. It was as if he was being given a vision of the future, the fourteen years between them suddenly stretching to make a huge and horrible difference. He would be a frail and cranky gent, such a burden and trial that eventually she would leave him for some younger fellow. He knew he could not bear it if this were the beginning of that end.

"Molly, I love you with all my heart," he said, stopping and placing one hand on her shoulder, the other raised to keep the tissue pressed against his bleeding head. The wind whipped around them, and a few gulls wheeled above them, screeching and yammering into the bright morning air.

"Arnica," she said, reaching up to dab his nose, and smiling. "I've just now remembered that's what you need. My sister gave me some and told me I should carry it in my bag when travelling. But you know, I was in such a hurry to pack, I'm sure it's still on the dresser at home. Look, let's get to the pharmacy. I'll bet you anything they give you some there, darling. You know, it's one of those homeopathic remedies to take after any shock. Jenny swears by it, she says it reduces swelling and bruising, she says it's amazing. I think it's a little yellow flower that grows in the hills in this part of France, actually. Isn't that funny?"

Arthur chose to see her concern as a kind of response to his declaration of love, for after all she was used to it—he told her every day, one way or another. But he wished, rather childishly, that she'd echoed his sentiment directly instead of coming out with the name of some damn plant. Arnica, yes, he'd believed he'd heard of it before. Jenny was always going on about the salubrious value of herbs and plants and, as Molly adored her older sister, their medicine cabinet was cluttered with bottles and vials of strange potions and powders.

Sure enough, no sooner had they arrived at the counter than the pharmacist suggested a "trauma dose" of arnica to be taken there on the spot, and also prescribed it for the next three days. Tiny white *pillules* to be left under the tongue until they dissolved and the medicine entered the bloodstream more quickly than through the digestive system. Arthur took the small plastic vial from the pharmacist, who showed him how to open it in such a way that his hands did not contaminate the contents, and let the little round things sit there, under his tongue, feeling the sweetness dissolve in a pleasant way. With water and cotton swabs the pharmacist cleaned his forehead and then used an antiseptic spray, which Arthur was told to use four times a day, instead of a bandage. Some aspirin for the inevitable headache, and advice to see a doctor if the pain became severe or if he felt like sleeping. "You must stay upright now for a few hours," she said, "but don't exert yourself."

"Well," said Arthur, as they went out into the busy street, "we'll have to tell Jenny about this, won't we? Let's go to that café over there and settle in for the morning, shall we? It seems to have a good view of the harbour." He was determined to be a good sport and not let this foolish injury spoil the occasion, but in fact his forehead throbbed and burned, and he felt oddly embarrassed by the stares of strangers.

Nevertheless, once they had ordered their coffees and croissants, he began to laugh, and Molly too. What a start to the day! What a shock it had been! Relaxed now, they both confided their most terrible fears: what would I *do* if you ever died like that? asked Molly. What would *I* do if you ever left me? asked Arthur. They leaned across the table and kissed each other tenderly.

They had lunch in a small restaurant, where Arthur had fresh anchovies on toast and entered into a complicated discussion with the proprietor about fishing history in this part of the Mediterranean compared with present-day activity. Late in the day, after some hours spent doing a tour of the Château Royal, and then sitting on the seawall behind the Église watching the waves crash and shatter, they began to wander the winding streets, poking about in souvenir shops, knowing they still had at least two hours to spend before restaurants would open at eight for dinner. At the top of a cul-de-sac they came across a small art gallery, brightly lit and welcoming, with a sign outside announcing a display of tapestries. Molly urged Arthur to come in with her, just for a minute. "You look tired, darling," she said. "Maybe there's a spot to sit down in here. Maybe you need to take more arnica too."

The tapestries turned out to be harshly modern and not pleasing to the eye. However, Arthur discovered a rack of canvases stacked against the wall, through which he began to browse. Within moments of his beginning to finger through the paintings, an attractive older woman in a smart black suit appeared by his side, smiling in a warm and winning fashion. Without doubt the owner of the gallery, she noted that *monsieur* must have a taste for art? *Monsieur* seemed to have been in an accident? She had Arthur in the palm of her hand in minutes, and Molly watched him succumb with fond amusement. The conversation became more animated: she waited, and yes, he told the woman that no, he was not European, he was from Canada.

The owner, predictably, feigned shock, and turned to include Molly in her performance. "But how is this possible?" she cried. "I assure you *Madame*, he sounds like one of us!"

Arthur winked at Molly, to let her know that he was not being taken in, but nevertheless, he began to look at paintings in earnest, requiring the woman to hold them up across the room, asking for information about the artists, consulting Molly for her opinion on every one. In English, Molly said, "Darling, shouldn't we be on our way?"

The woman in black gave her a cold eye. "I won't hear of you leaving now," she said, smiling warmly at Arthur. "It is the *heure de l'apéritif,* and I insist you must join me. Do you know the sweet wine from Banyuls? Perfect for this time of day. And I've already sent my assistant out for our usual plate of hors d'oeuvres. It is our custom here, *madame,* to relax and enjoy conversation." She smiled again, and left the room.

Having met her match, Molly shrugged and laughed, set down her bag and proceeded to look through a rack of watercolours and sketches, leaving Arthur to the oil paintings. In no time the woman returned with a tray of *beignets de morue,* small elegant wine glasses and a bottle of Banyuls. There was no doubt that she meant business, and since, on this off-season Saturday, fate had washed two likely buyers onto her shore, all she had to do was find the right painting. She knows our type, thought Molly, the sentimental North American with a penchant for romance. It's written all over us.

Luck was with the lady in black, for at the back of the rack lay a rather large canvas she had trouble removing, and so Arthur helped her get it out so they could lay it flat for a moment and decide whether it was worth viewing. From where she stood Molly could see it had been done in Fauve fashion, bright splashes of primitive colour, far too garish for her taste. But as Arthur asked the woman to take it across the room, she realized that the scene it portrayed was the very place they'd first walked arm in arm that morning, with Arthur's head dripping blood. The palm trees, the beach, the Catalan fishing boats pulled up on shore, the Église in the distance, the sparkling sea—there were even gulls.

"Plage du Port D'Avall," said the owner, her eyes focused on Arthur's face, moving in now with the excitement of the chase animating her sharp features. "An original, I assure you. Less painted than Plage Boromar, but a favourite with Matisse and with this fine artist, André Ricard, who of course knew Matisse well. Poor André, he's now so old, we fear that this may well be his last painting." Pause, just a beat, for some reflection. Standing back a little, not crowding him, then: "Does it please you, *monsieur?*"

Arthur turned to Molly, his face shining. "This is where we were when I told you I. . . ." He stopped, aware of the woman's presence and ability to speak English. "This is where we were when you told me I should take arnica," he said. "We will buy it, and we will call it *Arnica.*"

"Do you think so, darling?" asked Molly, trying to look at him in a meaningful way, to indicate that perhaps he had suffered a severe blow to the head and lost his mind. "Do you think we should ask how much it costs? And have we thought where we might hang it? And oh, darling, how will we get it home?"

Here, as the game had gone more quickly than she had anticipated, the woman was prepared to negotiate, and thus, within the next half hour, $2000 had been applied to Arthur's credit card account, and arrangements made for shipping the painting to Ottawa immediately, "entirely at my expense, *monsieur*, it is the least I can do."

They had a small party when the painting arrived, about a month after they had returned home. Molly invited Jerry and Rhonda and Ted, and Arthur had a few people come from his department, types who might be interested in "authentic art from the south of France." Molly sent out little invitations she made herself on which she wrote ARNICA PARTY so that Arthur would have the fun of explaining why they'd named the painting in this way. At the Glebe Apothecary on Bank Street she found small blue plastic vials of arnica, which she hung from ribbons around the room, little party favours for their guests to take home—magic, she said. Arthur ought to have had an enormous goose egg after his fall, and in fact had none. She found a recipe for *beignets de morue* ("it's just ground-up codfish," she told Jerry), and they ordered some bottles of Banyuls from Vintages, and it was really a very nice affair, everyone said afterwards. No one seemed to like the painting as much as Arthur did, but then he comforted himself with the truth that none of them had stood in that very place, with blood on his head, as he had.

The painting hangs now over the piano, and Molly is getting used to it, slowly, although its vibrant presence seems to her like a blast of trumpets in the tranquil blue of their living room. Still, the pleasure it gives Arthur is worth any amount of discomfort she might feel and, as time passes, she's found herself feeling rather affectionately toward the thing. Although she's sure that one of the framed postcards hung in their room at the hotel was exactly the same picture, she intends never to confide this to Arthur. What would be the point?

What a day that was! The gulls, the wind, the smell of the sea, everyone staring at them as they walked along that beach! But most of all she remembers her fear when she first saw Arthur fallen and flat, and she thinks of Arthur's face as she helped him from the sidewalk, so young and fearful too.

STARTING WITH THE CHAIR

My son is balancing on the edge of a rocking chair in the corner of my study with a thick red anthology of English literature on his knee, and he is telling me that these sonnets of Shakespeare's are really very good. He likes the way they always end in couplets—it makes him feel satisfied, he says. I am sitting at my desk, where I've been writing a letter until he knocked at the door, and am trying not to show my pleasure at this interruption, for at his age my approval annoys him. He does not want to be seen courting my good opinion, much as he wants it.

A small scene, infinitely expandable, endlessly rich in possibility. Lives ready to be unfurled from any point in the room, histories waiting to be explicated like unfolding Chinese boxes. Start anywhere.

Start with my son, Oliver, his dark curls so like his father's, falling down his forehead as he bends intently over the page, in love with Shakespeare and with English itself. He reads two sonnets aloud to prove to me how good they are, and he rolls the words around in his mouth as if they were large, sweet grapes. Those Italian ones, pale green and tasting of honey— we picked them from the vineyards ourselves the year we spent in Tuscany on my first sabbatical. Oliver was only a toddler then.

Or start with the old book from which he reads, my university text twenty-five years ago when I was studying literature and believing absolutely that someday I would be a poet too. Along the margins of the pages are scribbled notes and now-obscure references, drawings and doodles and brief but suggestive messages written to a young man who sat beside me in that first-year survey class. His name, apparently, was Jeffrey. From the look of these pages it is clear that I paid little attention to the material itself: in those days my interest was not so much in someone else's poems as in my own.

Oliver at fourteen shows much greater respect for what the past can offer and seems to have a genuine love of the printed word. But his real passion lies elsewhere: he wants to be a doctor, he says. A psychiatrist. That's probably the result of his seeing one now—a family therapist, really, but we decided it was essential during these past few months since Daniel's and my divorce became final and our living arrangements changed. Oliver seems to have transferred most of his affection and filial allegiance to the doctor, who explained to Daniel and me that this is a necessary process our son must go through in order to heal his legitimate hurt and anger at having his life disrupted.

I felt wounded by his tone and the way he said legitimate, as if he were subtly blaming us for upsetting Oliver, causing him such confusion and distress. But in fact he is a kindly man and only wants to see us all through this difficult time as well as he can. It will pass, the doctor promises. All this will pass.

Or the room in which we sit, where, outside the window, several enormous clumps of lavender are falling all over themselves with fragrant blossoms: but the latch is stuck and so we cannot open the window to catch the scent. We can only imagine it—as we do as soon as we think the word *lavender*. Which comes to mind first, Oliver and I asked ourselves over supper last week, the colour of lavender or the smell? We could not agree, and the argument took us through the breaded turkey and broccoli, right past salad to dessert. It is hard, sometimes, to find a topic of conversation to keep us both from staring at our plates and eating in silence, both of us deep in our dark and private thoughts. Neither of us speaks of missing Daniel, but we are aware of his absence, the empty chair. There is still hurt radiating out from the void where he once was: we are an amputated family suffering phantom pain.

Or the desk at which I am seated, its surface cluttered with papers and small objects, each one able to transform moment into memory. These things I carry from place to place, talismans against my own oblivion—the pebbles and feathers, the enamel pillbox, the sweet-grass basket full of shells, the china bowl, the small clay god, mouth puckered in a round *O* as if ready to whistle, whose eternal task it is to banish depression. Or so Daniel was told by an old lady in the Guatemalan market from whom he also bought a jade pendant to ward off indigestion and constipation: the stone left green marks on my clothes when I wore it on a chain around my neck.

Or the rocking chair on which my son, Oliver, sits. Yes, I like the idea of a chair as means of transport and means of entry into a story. The chair as engine, the chair as door, the chair as key.

Starting with the chair.

The padded seat is covered with floral needlepoint, giving the chair a much more elegant appearance than it had when first I was given it by my mother's sister, Auntie Glad. The covering then had been a drab orange fabric with a geometric design quite unsuitable for an old-fashioned chair. It was obviously a scrap of material brought home by Gladys from the textile factory where she often went to buy remnants for next to nothing. Her house filled itself over the years with homemade pillows and slipcovers and curtains in odd patterns and clashing colours: nothing matched, and that was as she liked it. She was an expansive, happy woman who took delight in a motley life—the unexpected bargains, the unforeseen pleasures.

My aunt kept the old chair in her home for more than twenty years because, although it had been left to my mother in my grandmother's will, it was not allowed in our house by my father, who detested rocking chairs. It was old, old enough that it was possibly valuable, but no one knew exactly where it had been made; there was some talk that it'd been brought over from Britain, but I think more likely it came from one of those small towns in Ontario where you see empty furniture factories nowadays. It had belonged to my great-grandmother who died on the family farm near Belleville at the beginning of the 20th century and that, rather than its status as an antique, gave the chair legendary ranking in our genealogy. The matriarch who founded our Canadian line had died in its embrace.

The chair is big, with such a wide berth that when it rocks it takes up a lot of space. My father's major argument against it was always its size (we don't have room for it, he'd say) whenever the subject came up. Which it didn't often, since my mother always favoured harmony over strife, and allowed that it was far more sensible to keep the chair at Glad's house since she lived only an hour away. There my mother could sit in it from time to time and enjoy rocking without any tension in the air. In her eyes there had been a nice compromise: in mine, however, the chair always looked like proof that my father had won and she had lost.

My mother remembered spending happy hours as a young girl curled up on the padded seat, which was large enough for her to pull her legs up underneath as she read. Whenever she described this scene, she portrayed herself with a novel in one hand and an apple in the other. It was a picture that intrigued me when I was a child because it seemed as if my mother were playing the role of Jo in *Little Women*, who was, of course, who I wanted to be. It was curiously unsettling to have both Jo and my mother in mind at the same time.

Although the chair is sufficiently broad for a small body to sprawl comfortably while reading, no adult locked within its encasing arms can do anything but sit up very straight against its firm, flat back. Slouching and slumping are out of the question. Which is how the chair tells us something about the upright character of the Welsh-born lady who died in it: she must have had her old spine rigid against the wooden back even as she drew her last breath, for when they found her she was sitting with her hands folded in her lap, as stiff and righteous in death as she'd been in life.

Actually, it wasn't "they" who found her, it was Janet, the hired girl she'd employed only that spring (my great-grandmother died in November). Janet came from a recently landed Scottish family on a neighbouring farm down the concession, and had taken good care of the sick woman all during the summer, quietly watching her stubborn grasp on life weaken. Janet never let on what she thought—that the old lady was going to die soon— to any of her employer's children or grandchildren when they came to visit, nor did she impart her concern that she'd soon be out of a job. She had faith, did Janet, that something would happen to save her.

The day my great-grandmother passed on had been a busy one for Janet, making raisin bread and lemon pie and two kinds of cake to serve when Ethel Walpole, wife of the Methodist minister, came for her regular Tuesday afternoon "keeping company." Mrs. Walpole was a stout, good-hearted soul who liked a little something with her tea, and Janet always obliged by laying out a fine tray of baked goods from which she could choose. That day, the reverend's wife had spent her hours in sociable silence, as the elderly are wont to do, sitting by the parlour woodstove and crocheting, knitting, doing a bit of mending as well. Simply being present, needle in hand.

Janet saw Mrs. Walpole to the front door just as the clock in the hall struck five, and after clearing up the tea things she'd come into the room to stoke up the waning fire in the stove. Then she'd gone to the window and pulled the heavy drapes against the night, noting there was a thin line of cold blue light still on the horizon. It made her think of all the months of winter darkness yet ahead, she said.

After she'd done that, singing softly to herself, as she did continually to fill the silent rooms with the sound of a voice, she'd gone over to arrange a woollen shawl around those frail and ailing shoulders. It was perfectly normal for my great-grandmother to sit wordlessly, dreaming by the fire, so that didn't trouble Janet; she kept on singing as she always did and went off to the kitchen, where she washed the teacups and got supper ready. It was nearly an hour later when she came back into the room to waken the old woman and bring her to the table for her nightly soup. When Janet touched the hands resting in her lap, she cried out in alarm, for the fingers were stiff and cold.

Janet was inconsolable, blaming herself for not being with her mistress at the moment of departure from this world, for having let her die alone in the room. "All alone, with never another soul to see her out," she said, over and over. She wept and howled and it seemed would never be comforted: luckily, my great-uncle Howard, still single at forty and the youngest of the deceased's five living children, arrived late that night from town, where he was a senior partner in a small law firm, and he took it upon himself to offer solace to Janet in the pantry while the rest of the family were organizing things in the parlour.

When, some months later, it became evident that Uncle Howard's charitable efforts would bear fruit, he and young Janet were married by Reverend Walpole in his front sitting room, and Janet became my mother's favourite aunt. I remember her as a very old lady, speckled all over like a wild bird's egg, and with a sharp little face that always looked slightly injured and put out. She was not well educated, and in a family such as ours where pride was taken in academic accomplishments—it was how one left the farm, after all— poor Janet was forever scorned and until her dying day referred to, behind her back, as "the help." Howard progressed in life—in spite of Janet, his sisters and brothers and their children all said. Only my mother liked her and stuck up for her. Janet just never had a chance to get away to school, she said, and that was Howard's fault if it was anyone's. She claimed that Howard had little gumption and that it was entirely through Janet's efforts he eventually became a judge.

It was from Janet that the story of the chair originally came, and it may have been because of her fondness for her aunt that my mother felt such a strong nostalgic attachment to a piece of furniture, for ordinarily she was not a sentimental woman. She would tell and retell Janet's tale as if it were her own, as if it were she herself who had found her dead grandmother. My mother's mother—Howard's sister—had inherited the chair, perhaps because she was the eldest of the five: when she died, they found she'd written on a slip of paper, stuck in the corner of her dressing table mirror, that her daughter Gwen was to have "the old padded rocker, the one Granny died in."

And then, years later, my mother, Gwen, died unexpectedly and far too young, and Auntie Glad said to me at the funeral, "Now, child, you'll have her chair." No longer a child—by then, I was an assistant professor in the comparative literature department, had been married to Daniel for five years and was noticeably pregnant with Oliver—I couldn't think for a moment what she meant, until she made the movement of rocking back and forth. "It'll be a grand place to suckle the baby," she added, looking pointedly at my swollen abdomen. "That straight back will give you good support and the arms are the right height for your elbows too, mark my words. You and that husband of yours drive up and get it as soon as you can."

Unlike my father who was so clear about what he liked and disliked, Daniel is a man of loosely held opinion, letting notions run carelessly through his life like glass beads through an Arab trader's fingers. If I liked the big chair and wanted it in our house, it was all the same to him, he said. Personally, he found it a bit grotesque, but maybe that was only on account of the awful fabric. We could change that easily, but it was up to me.

Life was always like that with Daniel, during our years of marriage: his slight removal from, and disavowal of, whatever I liked or wanted or believed in, and then his passive acceptance. Yes, have it, by all means. I'd never prevent you from having what you want, or thinking what you want. What kind of guy do you take me for, anyway? Easygoing laughter, acquiescence and a gentle indifference that I believed for too many years was a kind of love.

Of course Auntie Glad was right—I did nurse Oliver in that chair, for the enclosure of the back and arms provided a firm frame within which to experience the strange sensation of his sweet, tiny mouth pulling fiercely at my nipple. Sometimes the feeling would be so sharp that I'd imagine my entire body was going to splinter itself around the room, and it was only the old chair holding me together and keeping me from flying apart. From the joy of motherhood or the pain? Who knows?

Oliver is our only child, Daniel's and mine. I feel as if I have let my family down by not having a daughter

to whom to pass the chair, and I am glad that big jolly
Aunt Glad and little freckled Great-Aunt Janet are
dead and gone so that they don't have to know our
female line is dwindling. Of course, neither of them
would ever have said a word to make me feel bad
about this, but they would have felt quietly sad.
I know it, and I grieve on their account as well as
on my own.

But the way things have turned out, it's been
better having only one kid to call himself—ruefully
and with some humour—"the product of a broken
home." We have shared custody, and Oliver divides
his time and heart evenly between us—us and the
doctor, that is. I understand his attachment. I've been
going to a therapist too, these past few years, although
not the same one. I began a few years ago, around
the time that Daniel brought back the small clay god,
hoping with that gesture to make me smile, to force
me to forgive him for going to Guatemala in the
first place.

We both acted as if what had happened was only a
quarrel over principles—I disagreed with his doing
business in that country at that time and he, typically,
said that his deals (importing native crafts to Toronto)
were nothing to do with politics. As if money could
change hands in Guatemala without that being a
political act! In truth, I had been increasingly depressed
about how little we understood each other well before

this trip, and I found myself sinking deeper into gloom with each new event that proved me right. We were on different sides, it was clear.

But the clay god did make me laugh, and I was genuinely touched by his wanting me to feel better and to be myself again. I would sit in the old rocking chair, enclosed and safe, and try to remember how we had fallen in love, hoping that if I could figure *that* out we could manage to keep on going and love each other again. I wanted to stay married at the same time as I was clearly and increasingly miserable. When I was feeling especially low, I would think of my great-grandmother, wishing that I too could simply give up the ghost as I rocked. Nothing overtly suicidal, you understand. Just that sense of giving up that is deeper than apathy, worse than anger. And it eventually passed. This too, says the doctor, will pass.

Oliver and I have lived here without Daniel since last year, and the new arrangement suits me well. I have finished the book of poems I began years ago, and with luck it will be published later this fall. My contract, with a small regional press, is never going to make me famous but at least respectable, and acknowledged as a poet, a real poet, after all this time. Naturally, being a perfectionist whose field is language, I am still fine-tuning some of the poems, and it is an interminable process, for I am always capable of finding another word to alter or remove.

The problem is usually Daniel. Not his direct interference, of course, or even his name, but a word here or a phrase there that evokes his face, the sound of his voice, the way he would lean back with his arms folded behind his head when he was listening, which meant he wasn't really listening at all. I find that the intense blue of his eyes seems to crop up everywhere—in one poem the sky, in another (about a young girl running away from home) the colour of a passing car. Somehow, his physical presence makes its way unbidden into every poem. No matter that I want these poems to be pure, or to believe myself to be creating them from language undefiled by remembrance, I find Daniel emerging, and taking over.

You see here, for example. All sources flow to the same end as all rivers run into the sea. No matter which object in the room we might have chosen, I have only one story to tell, and there is only one end to the story.

One day our marriage came apart as Daniel, sitting on the edge of the bed pulling on his socks, said that I must believe that it was nothing personal but it was finished. It, whatever *it* was, whatever it had been that was us. "Honestly, nothing personal," he said again, reaching for me as I scuttled like a wounded insect across the bed away from him. I was stricken, not with shock or sadness, but with rage—rage at myself for having tried too long to stay in love with him, and rage that it was Daniel, ever the slippery prevaricator, the laid-back procrastinator, Daniel who had dared first speak the truth.

My son leans back now in the rocking chair with a sigh of deep satisfaction, having read the last two lines of Sonnet 30. The chair makes a gasping, creaky sound and then the room is suddenly very still, as if every object in it had suddenly drawn breath, and I look down at the letter (an impersonal letter dealing with a forgotten insurance policy) that I've been writing to Daniel, and tears come to my eyes. Oliver will be entirely fed up with me if he thinks his recitation has made me emotional, and so I keep my head down for a long time, as if contemplating Shakespeare's genius.

My inky words before me on the ivory-coloured paper swim and blur, and I pull myself together only by thinking of the old rocking chair, which leads me to plucky little Janet, her back firmly wedged against the corner of the pantry shelf, lifting her skirts for Howard. A spunky survivor, that Janet. There's a lesson there.

Oliver rises from the chair and closes the old *College Survey* with a snap. "What would have happened if you'd gone off with this Jeffrey?" he says, and in his awkward, adolescent way puts his hand on my hair in what purports to be a comradely pat. "This person you wrote notes to, in the margins," he adds.

"Ah, he was never a serious candidate," I say, raising my head again and ready to banter in the way
we've developed during these months. "He was only
marginal, Oliver."

But nothing is marginal, is it? Not the book, nor
the old rocking chair, nor the letter to the father of
my son, nor the sound of sonnets being read aloud as
the sun is streaming through the window. Nor the
lavender outside, strung all over with bees. It is all
history, and it is all here in every present moment.
Everything belongs right where it is. There is nothing
in our lives that doesn't fit.

The whole spectrum of fictional possibility includes the infra-red of pure history and the ultra-violet of pure imagination . . . and in between we can distinguish many shades of coloration . . . But all are fragments of the white radiance of truth which is present in both history books and fairy tales but only partly present in each—fragmented by the prism of fiction without which we should not be able to see it at all. For truth is like ordinary light, present everywhere but invisible, and we must break it to behold it.

Robert Scholes, The Elements of Fiction

Some of these essays and stories have appeared in earlier and different versions. "Rain" (Ottawa, 1982) was first broadcast as a letter to Peter Gzowski in 1982 and later published in *The Morningside Papers* (McClelland & Stewart Ltd., 1985). "There Is No Word for Home" was first published in *BRICK*, number 65–66 / Fall 2000, and excerpted in *Utne Reader*, March / April, 2001. "Saving Stones" was first published as *How I Got Started and Why I Can't Stop*, a chapbook in the Magnum Readings Series (Ottawa, 1993) and later abbreviated in *Into the Nineties* (Kunapipi Press, 1994). In yet another version, it has appeared in *Femmes et Ecriture* (Éditions Kaledioscope, 2002). "Going to Banaue" was published as "Notes from the Philippines" in the PEN anthology *Writing Away* (McClelland & Stewart Ltd., 1994). "Starting with the Chair" was also first published in *Into the Nineties*. "The Window" was first published in the *Ottawa Citizen*, July 2001.

Grateful acknowledgment is made to the following for permission to reprint previously published material:

The quote from the essay "The Morality of Things" by Bruce Chatwin comes from the collection called *Anatomy of Restlessness: Selected Writings, 1969–1989*, Penguin Books USA Inc., New York, 1996. Copyright © 1996 The Legal Representative of C.B. Chatwin.

The quote from the essay "Clutter" by Adam Phillips is from his collection called *Promises, Promises*, Faber & Faber, London, 2000.

The quote by Robert Scholes is from *The Elements of Fiction*, Third Canadian Edition, edited by Robert Scholes and Rosemary Sullivan, Oxford University Press, Toronto, 1994.

The quote from Margaret Avison's poem "From a Provincial" is from *Winter Sun*, University of Toronto Press, Toronto, 1962.

The quote from Jan Zwicky's poem "Transparence" is from *Songs for Relinquishing the Earth*, Brick Books, London, 1998.

The quote from Don McKay's essay "Baler Twine" is from *Vis à Vis*, Gaspereau Press, Kentville, 2001.

The quote from Michael Ondaatje's novel is from Hana's letter in *The English Patient*, McClelland & Stewart Ltd., Toronto, 1992.

A NOTE ABOUT THE AUTHOR

Isabel Huggan grew up in small-town Ontario, an experience
that shaped her prize-winning first book, *The Elizabeth Stories*,
which established her as an original, talented writer. In 1987
her husband's work took the family to Kenya and she has
found herself living abroad ever since—a situation reflected in
You Never Know, a second collection of stories. Her work has
been published in the United States, Great Britain, France,
Spain, Holland and Italy. She still returns each year to Canada
from her home in France.

A NOTE ABOUT THE TYPE

Belonging is typeset in a digitized form of "Fournier," originally designed and cut in the mid-sixteenth century in Paris by Simon Pierre Fournier, one of Europe's most influential type artists of the time. By the turn of the twentieth century, Fournier, along with its contemporary "Garamond," were considered the pre-eminent serif faces for book text throughout France. The original matrices were recut by the Monotype Corporation in 1925.